Thriving

Quin

Catalog-in-Publication Data for this book available from the Library of Congress.

ISBN 978-0-578-80336-4

DEDICATION

I'd like to dedicate this book to all my family, my friends, and in particular, all of my YouTube subscribers. I am very grateful that I have the opportunity to tell my story to thousands of people who have given me their ears and support. I would also like to express how honored I am to be a part of everyone's recovery in the narcissistic survivor community who have healed from the knowledge that I have shared with them. This dedication is my way to recognize all the people who have made a big difference in my life. I've learned a lot from all of your stories and experiences, and I'm thankful forever.

TABLE OF CONTENTS

Introduction

I was convinced that you should treat others the way you wanted to be treated, and in return, others would give back the same way you did. But going through life, I have seen too many situations where those principles have not been reciprocated. In fact, I've seen the opposite happen many times. Have you ever heard of the saying, "Give someone an inch and they're going to try to take a mile???"That old saying became ever so true as I grew older and wiser.

Your kindness is often taken for weakness and being naive. Giving people the benefit of doubt is merely a false sense of security, in an attempt to reduce the fears of knowing that cold-hearted and evil individuals in the world who enjoy preying on the morally sound and the weak exist. I don't think anyone would really relish the idea that they are actually people who get off on hurting and taking advantage of people who are kind and generous or who live in any other kind of wholesome way. The mere fact that people like this exist among us in society is quite alarming.

At some point in our lives, we are bound to encounter one of these predatory types of individuals, and when we do, if we cannot properly identify and respond to take care of ourselves or take the right measures to limit our interactions with them, you can be assured that at some point you will be a victim of the circumstance to a calculated, cold-hearted person. The mental and psychological effects of such encounters can leave a person emotionally damaged for life, triggering post-traumatic stress within the psyche of an individual. Some people may never recover from these traumatic events of being victimized over and over again. Post-Traumatic Stress Disorder is typical for survivors, but it doesn't always have to be that exact reason.

Maya Angelou once said, "When someone shows you who they are, believe them for the first time." No truer words could have been spoken by the great Maya Angelou. When any person displays any disdainful characteristics about themselves without taking into account how they may be perceived by you or how they may be committing acts which may harm you, it is a clear indication that this normal behavior which lacks empathy from the abuser. Even more so, human nature dictates that if a person does something more than once, it is likely to stem from a pattern of behaviors that have been carried out over and over again, turning into a habit that eventually becomes part of their character.

In my life experience, I've learned to vet people on the basis of merit, because giving people the benefit of the doubt is something that I no longer subscribe to. Instead, I'm focus on seeing the patterns in people's behavior. Repetitive behavior is without correction is not coincidental. It's coming from repetition and will undoubtedly be hard to change. I was naive and foolishly entering into relationships and situations by giving the benefit of doubt, and believing that when a person strongly professed that they were the real deal and wanted to have a meaningful connection with me, they really intended to on making those necessary efforts in order to honor their word. But I was wrong. It wasn't until I found myself in a situation with one of those toxic individuals myself that made me look at life and interact with people in a completely different way, and from that day forward, I wouldn’t be the same again.

Chapter 1: The Encounter

My initial encounter with her was at work on the summer of 2013. She appeared somewhat decent to me at first. She was very attractive, dark brown eyes, Milky Way chocolate skin and a smile that was so bright and beautiful that it could dim the light of the sun. I was definitely attracted to her and wanted to put myself in a better position of getting to know her. But I could not really press the situation because I wasn't necessarily comfortable with dating someone who I worked with. I fell back on that idea of shooting my shot at her until I had time to observe her a bit at work. One of the things that was impressive to me about her was that her work ethic was impeccable; very rarely did she take off or miss any day for that matter. Plus, she seemed to be a loner, no friends and wasn't up in anyone's business. She was just a hard-consistent worker. For me, that spoke volumes and got my undivided attention.

As weeks went by and me playing like I didn't notice her, trying to appear disinterested, I made my move. I approached her. I remember her disposition being friendly and pretty down to earth. Hell! She even offered me some of her pizza that day at lunch when I decided to walk up to her. “Are you dating anyone?” I asked. “No, not right now”, she replied. Okay…Well maybe we can hang out sometime whenever our days off matches.

“That would be nice”, she replied. “Take my number”.

I obliged and saved it into my phone.

Later on, that evening, I remember her sending me a text message. As I started reading the text I noticed that it was her. She said, “Hey! “ I smiled when I saw it saying to myself – okay, she’s interested. She made the first move pretty early. I responded back: “hey,”

She replied just saying “Hi, what are you doing”.

I responded with “nothing much, just winding down for the evening and getting ready for bed”.

“Okay, well in that case I will just see you tomorrow” she replied.

I replied “okay, that sounds good. Have a good night”.

I remember our first time actually hanging out. It was on a weekend and we linked up and went out to play pool. It was a pretty chill evening. We played pool on the table. I remember I had to go to a restroom and when I came back, the balls on the table had been rearranged for her to easily get her shots to go in without effort. I said "Hey, did you try to set this up so that you can get an easy win on me or something (laughing)?" she got offended right away at first and she said "no, why would you think that? I am not a cheater. This is the balls on the table were before you left".

Now, I knew the balls had been moved. I am no dummy and I was definitely not seeing things, but she insisted. I thought she was just being playful. So, I shrugged it off and didn't make much of it laughing. She ended up winning of course, because she had prearranged and placed the balls in position so that she could easily get to win. At that point, I just continued to laugh at the situation. I noticed that she wasn't really laughing. She stayed serious. Nonetheless, I didn't make a big deal out of it; it was our first time hanging out and I wanted the evening to end well. So I didn't harp on it too much, I just to let it go.

As we were walking to my car which at the time, she asked what kind of car it was and I said a Nissan Ultima 2013. It's brand new and pretty decent to me I said.

"Naah, it's not all that. That shit is basic as hell to me" she said.

I was like "wow... okay. I see you are pretty critical on things."
"No, just stating a fact" She replied.

This time, I was getting turned off by her attitude. I still shrugged to calm it off at the time like she's just joking. I'm pretty confident in myself so it was cool. I am a funny guy at times so I thought maybe she was low-key hating in a playful way. We headed back to her house to drop her off.

One thing that stood out for me, looking back on that evening was when we pulled up to her apartment. There were speed bumps that were in the drive way. And as I drove over one of speed bumps, my soda cap fell down from the center console of the arm rest in the car. It fell on her side, down towards the floor mat at her feet. As I reached over to pick up the cap, she made a remark saying "don't touch me" very firmly as though I was trying to grab her feet. Now, mind you, she had seen the cap fall prior to me reaching down to grab it and there was no need for her to actually assume that I was reaching out to grab her feet. Yet, she made the statement "don't touch me".

"Wow! You are pretty dramatic. Why would I be reaching out for your feet?" I asked.

She never replied and instead abruptly took off her seat belt, opened the car door and got out. I watched her walk away from my car to her apartment. In my head, I thought that this chick is kind of weird. That situation didn't sit well with me and to be honest, it made me feel uncomfortable about being around her again.

When the work week started again, she approached me and greeted me with that beautiful smile. I hesitantly replied "Hi!

"You brought launch today? Are you eating out?" she asked.

In my head I thought: "You acted really shady in our last time hanging out and didn't even say thank you for any of the time that I spent with you or for anything that I did with you that evening and you just walked off like I wasn't even there. And now, you are cool, calm and collected like none of that happened, and you want to hang out for launch?"

Nonetheless, I rationalized it as maybe it was just one of them days like that Monica song, back in the day and I said to myself "she might be a really cool girl to get to know. Maybe it's just that getting to know each other stage that has to be ironed out. This kind of thing does tend happen when you're first getting to know someone new. So, I said "I going to go out to eat lunch today".

She said "oh, okay! I got launch on me then."

"Okay" I responded.

We ended up going to a mom & pop shop not too far from work for launch. We sat outside to eat. I asked the usual questions that a normal person would ask whenever they first meet someone. Like- "how long have you been single and what happened with your last relationship?

She replied "I have been single for about a year. I have dated other guys but they were lame. My ex really messed me up in my head. He was abusive to me. He put me down a lot and I have been through this with him for nine years. I suffered the whole time. The things that he did to me were indescribable"

"How old are you", I asked.

"Twenty-seven" she answered.

"ohm… okay" I said "so it was in your younger years that you went through this".

She said "Yes".

She then goes on to talk about how people always tried to use her. She has a heart of gold but people never seem to appreciate her, including her family which she moved completely out of the state from where they lived.

"Wow" I said to her. "That's pretty drastic to move completely to another state with no family or friends just completely on your own".

"Yeah, I needed a change in scenery and I wanted to go somewhere I can focus and have a fresh start without any distractions' she said.

As I was listening to her, I had the look of disbelief on my face because I felt that she was leaving some details out about her past situation. I guessed she noticed it on my face that I had this blatant of look of disbelief. She tried to divert the conversation though, and asked me where I got my haircut from. She said it looks really good.

"You must have a good barber and you are very handsome" she remarked.

She then went on to say "I bet you talk to a lot of girls at work too".

I replied "not really; I have a barber. I keep myself up and I try to look as decent as possible. That's the way I was raised. It's false when you think that I have a lot of girls at work that I'm talking to. Why would you think that? I am just a regular guy; Plus, I am not trying to build a reputation of some guy that is trying to holla at all the women at their job. Well, you sure did come to holla at me". I walked up to you because I saw some specific qualities in you that I found very attractive. It caught my attention and it motivated me enough to come speak to you".

"Oh really? Sounds like what any other guys would say" she said." We better get back to work".

Anyway, for the next few weeks that we were hanging out together. We went to places like the mall, we did happy hour together, laughing, joking and spending a lot of time talking on the phone. Everything seemed cool. That initial meeting, we had almost seemed like it was a misunderstanding, because now things are flowing pretty nice. It was starting to develop into a pretty good friendship. So, I thought at least.

I remember one 4th of July, we decided to hang out and go out of town and watch the fireworks. I decided to plan a nice type of evening for the both of us. We were going to stay in the hotel room and be out of town and return after the weekend or after the holiday at least. I was pretty anxious and excited. We were going to be on a small type of road trip which was at least two hours away and since this was going to be our very first time

spending a lot of time together in a more intimate setting. I felt that this would be a really good test of seeing how well we actually interact under circumstances of this kind.
We prepared some food before going- we had burgers, some chicken, potato salad and drinks. We were really ready to have a good time. I picked her up, loaded the car and we headed off about two hours north in the direction of where we were to watch the 4th of July fireworks. We had a blast that 4th of July watching the fireworks. That whole evening was amazing to me.

In the morning as I awoke, she was already up getting dressed ready to go get breakfast. She asked me if I wanted anything.

"Something light, nothing heavy. Some muffins, juice, fruits... that would do for me" I said.

That's about all that you could get at this hotel anyway. They didn't serve full breakfast. I noticed she left with her book bag. I was going into the bathroom when she said she would be right back. When she finally returned, she had that muffin that I asked for and a yogurt and an

orange in her hand; then she takes off her book bag and then she pulls out like six yogurts, several muffins, ten oranges and all sort of all those jelly packs. I asked her with a chuckle "why did you grab all that stuff as if no one else in the hotel might want anything for themselves?" She replied that most of the times, this stuff just goes to waste anyway. My eyebrows rose and in response I said "Okay, if you say so".
"How is this girl really living? She is acting like a scavenger that doesn't have anything and is basically in survival mode. Something is off with this" I thought to myself. I didn't dwell too much on it at that time.

As we were headed back from our little get away holiday on the highway listening to music. She turns the music down and out of the blues she asks "what do you want with me?"

I said "what do I want with you? Well I am trying to get to know you and see if things can develop into something more official."
She laughed out loud saying "really? You sure about that? I am a handful Quinn". "What do you mean by that?" I asked.
She smiled at me and turned the music back up. I looked over and said "let's see what happens then"

Interpretation

Every first encounter will immerse as it is designed to be a mystery. First of all, the narcissist had the advantage because they are operating out of a fictitious made up character, while you are being genuine and revealing things about yourself in which the narcissist will definitely use against you.

This initial encounter is also critical to define formulation and customization of the false character by way of love bombing. Love bombing is getting you to like them but not be too sure where you stand with them at the same time. But its constant interaction and stimulation of unprecedented levels of compliments, and different types of admiration to seduce you.

This is all used in the beginning so that you get very fond of them being in your company. You'll desire to be around them because of the way they make you feel. As this builds, and as you start to fantasize about how you love to be around them and how much you would love to have more of them, the narcissist basically allows you to fall right into their trap.

Chapter 2: The Love Bombing

At this point in time, it's been a little over three weeks of getting to know this girl I met at work and now we are supposedly taking it to the next level. We are starting to make a relationship out of this and it is becoming more official. This courting period was unlike any that I have ever experienced. I was getting showered with compliments about how much of a man I was and unlike anyone she had ever met before in her life. Don't get it twisted, I wasn't just buying into this for her to let this barraging of compliments about me go to my head, but it did feel good to hear it coming from her.

I can recall one time when we were talking on phone and she mentioned to me that she doesn't mind giving me compliments because she liked that I was attractive to her. She told me that she needs plenty of validation herself and she can be a bit needy at times, but nothing overboard. She seemed to at times come up with these tad bits and pieces about herself in out of place moments. Then she would switch back up and make the conversation all about me again talking about how special and lucky she was to have met a guy like me.

Initially, at that time she would always follow it up with an act of kindness, either making me lunch or catering to me with. It really felt good. She would ask what type of things that I was into and I would tell her the kind of hobbies and things that I liked. For instance, if I talked about racing cars because I am very much into muscle cars and racing. Once she knew what I liked. She would then go to research and study the very thing that I told her, and then familiarize herself with it. And then she would try to do something that was in sync with what I liked. For example, by liking racing cars, she will find, television shows about racing and she would go into the same mode of enjoyment that I had for it. She would have the same passion for it as well. Tell me how I could be a good race driver too" she would ask. "You are a good driver and you make me feel really comfortable driving" she would say.

This could seem like support, and I did not think about it in a suspicious way at the time because maybe she was just that into me and she really did want to support me in that way. At the time, I thought it was her way of showing genuine interest for the things that I was interested in. it was quite refreshing, but it did seem somewhat fake to me at the same time too. Nevertheless, I made myself okay with it for the time being.

After about two months, she started to raise her level of seduction with me. She began to invite me over to her place for sexual activities whenever her roommate was gone. These sexual activities were unlike normal sexual activities because of the intensity, passion and how active she would get into it. It was like very strong and filled with a lot of lust. It was high intensity sexual encounters for sure. We were going at it like cats and dogs. It seemed like she was always in the mood and would freakily mention how much she loved sex. There were a lot of home cooked meals drawn into the mix as well, with full body massages and of course more sex.

I am also an avid fan of football and basketball which when the game was on, she would make me feel like I was at a tail gate, except that this was indoors. She would grill hotdogs; get chips and an assortment of snacks to make me feel as comfortable as possible while watching the game. On top of that, she would sit and watch the whole game with me. I would think to myself like "wow! This is the perfect chick." She was so accommodating.

She made sure I was at the center of her attention and all I had to do was to compliment her and give her praise. Of course, I would do more than that. I would try to reciprocate and do nice things for her as well. I would try to match whatever she was putting out. She would always say "this is what a woman is supposed to do for her man. Any woman who couldn't didn't deserve a man like me". She had all the right answers at that time. I was being rocked to sleep and I didn't even know it. But that would soon be coming to an end. This honeymoon love stage couldn't last for long as the first red flag incident was about to happen.

I can remember coming home from a 12-hour shift, tired as hell and beaten from a long day of work. I took a shower and I ate the food she had prepared. We would spend time on and off at each other's place, but this time she was at mine. It was time to go to bed, me being sleepy as hell, I had to get to work early in the morning again. As I was trying to go to sleep, she was trying to have sex. I wasn't up for it though, yet she persisted and started kissing on my neck and shoulders and my lips. As we were lying down, mind you, I am half way asleep at this point and she is trying to get her (9.40) off. She mounts me and is kissing my lips even more. Then all of a sudden, she gets upset and very angrily said "who the fuck is Tina".

I am looking at her puzzled like what the hell is this girl talking about. Then she says again "are you talking to some bitch named Tina? You just called me another bitch's name".

At that point I am like "woe… what the hell? I didn't even open my mouth to say anything whole-time.

"Yes, you did call me another bitch's name" she replied.

At this point, I am pissed because I had about seven hours of sleep to get before I had to get up again and I am being accused and arguing with this girl about calling her another female's name, which I did not do.
She goes into a cursing frenzy even more, yelling at me "Oh my God, I can't believe you are fucking with another bitch."

I replied and said "seriously? You really gonna play this out? This is really ridiculous you've got to be kidding me? You know what? I am not going to do this with you. Stay in here I'm sleeping in the living room. I don't have time for this I am getting some rest. You are going to be gone in the morning and you are not going come back here again" I said.

As I walked to the living room, she walks up to me and said calmly which really confused me and said, "I will stop. Maybe I heard wrong in my mind and I overreacted. Please don't make this big more than what it is. I am sorry".

I said "what?"

"I got in my feelings because I felt rejected by you and made it all up. I am sorry. I am just really sensitive and I get that way sometimes" she told me." A lot of things happen in my past relationships that sometimes make me get flashbacks when certain things happen"

At this point, I am thinking to myself like "you've got to be kidding me. All of this shit is causing a scene and a big argument all for nothing? Just because she felt slighted by her ego not being validated?"

This is crazy! I have never experienced anything like it before. I just couldn't let it rest and I told her "hey! Look, if you are unhealed and you react to things like this that trigger you then we are not going to work out."

She said "no I am sorry. I won't let it happen again. I just overreacted and blew it out of proportion. I was wrong and I promise I won't do it again. I won't bother you; I will let you get your rest."

I reluctantly went back to the room, got into the bed and laid down. I was so tired and fell asleep right away.

Upon waking up in the morning to the unmistakable smell of bacon, I get myself up and glanced into the kitchen and noticed her making breakfast. She walked into the room and said "I made you some breakfast". She is positioned directly in front of me and she takes both of her hands and grabs my hands gently and says "I am sorry about last night. I overreacted and I am really sorry though. I feel foolish. Let's go eat" she says.

I am completely taken back by this because just last night there was this raging devil in this girl insisting that I called her some other woman's name and then this morning it's like nothing ever happened. I have to tell you that eating breakfast that morning wasn't the best time, compared to other times that we have had before. It felt pretty awkward in fact.

As I was eating, I was still trying to figure out how someone would act completely out of order and make something up so drastic. I begin to feel that something may not be alright with this girl and I am sure my demeanor showed it as well. She probably sensed that I had thoughts of concern on my mind about her and it would definitely bring some changes on my end.

Interpretation

When you first meet a narcissist and they go this love bombing phase of getting the new to fall for them, they are pulling out all the bells and whistles and there is a lot of passionate encounters, there is a lot of sex, a lot of uninhabited thing that they will do for you to really make you directly focused on them to ensure that your attention is not drawn anywhere else. This is a mask! It is not real. It is a covering to make you feel like you have met your soul mate or you have met the right person.

They are doing everything, they like everything you like; they are going along with everything you approve of with no resistance at first. This is one of the reasons why I said you can get easily rocked asleep if you are not paying attention. If you are so caught up in the wonderful things they are doing and all the fun that you are having with them, you can easily get overwhelmed with this type of treatment from them and be addicted to it. That is the whole point; to get you addicted to them. Being with a person that just would go above and beyond to please you; you have to understand that to whom much is given, much is required and you would have to pay for all of these things they are doing. It is not coming from a genuine place. It is all a strategy and it will be used against you later.

Chapter 3: Crazy Making, Let the Games Begin!

The first day after that argument, things wouldn't quite be the same again. As I begin to clear my mind from the fog of this girl being a sweet and accommodating person, I started to wonder if I had a problematic individual on my hands. I gave her the benefit of the doubt though and I believed that she was really sorry, because of some past issues and was indeed trying to work on them. At this point, she is coming over to my house more and more and it's the typical getting ready for bed routine. I usually set my alarm clock on my phone and set it next to my pillow. As I am going to sleep, talking to her and letting her know that I would see her at work tomorrow.

Mind you my shift starts two hours earlier than hers. I told her that I was going to bed; she says "okay, do you need me to make anything for you in the morning?

I said "no, I think I will grab something at work tomorrow". After that conversation, I went to sleep and began to doze off with my phone next to me.

In the morning, I can remember her saying “Bae! Bae! Don’t you have to get up? It’s after seven.

I used to wake up at about 6:45 to give myself sometime before heading out to work. But today, I am already fifteen minutes behind. I immediately reached for where my phone was and it wasn’t there. I said “where is my phone?” I could have sworn that I put it next to me before I went to bed and lay down. I began to move the pillows around, looking under the bed and I couldn’t find it. Anyway, I could not spend too much time looking for it because I was running late already. As I was getting together, she comes to me and says “Bae, come here”. She walked me into the kitchen and she pointed to the refrigerator next to the counter and said, “Look” shaking her head, there’s your phone still on the charger. You probably forgot to get it last night when you were going to bed.”

I am thinking like “No! No! No! I didn’t leave my phone here “I was pretty tired though, but did I? No, there’s no way. Did I get up? Did I mistake something this time?” I was thinking that this is strange. I kept wondering if I really did leave it there.

I couldn't dwell on that too much because I was running late. I put those thoughts aside, got dressed and left for work. I called her later and asked her "did you move my phone?"

"Why would I move your phone, I don't touch your stuffs. You were probably just tired and you forgot" she replied.

I cooled off again but I felt uneasy with that answer because my mind was saying "no, you didn't put your phone by the refrigerator last night on the charger". Another part of me was rationalizing it in a state of confusion saying "maybe you did this time. Maybe you were tired and just forgot". But I wasn't all the way done going through that in my mind. It just didn't sit well with me. I said to myself "that damn girl probably moved it" but then I kept going back and forth on my head and my logic was saying "but that wouldn't make any sense for anyone to do that, she knows you had to get up and go to work. Why would she deliberately try to make you late for work? Her shift starts two hours after your shift; it doesn't make sense for her to want to see you not get to work on time. So, I left that thought alone.

It wasn't until our next trip out of town, only just having our get away. We lodged in the hotel. In our hotel room, again at night while we were lying down in the bed (this particular bed was a sleep number bed with which you can adjust the firmness of the bedding). I was on the bed already. She has the sleep number controller on her side. I am starting to fall asleep and I notice myself sinking into the bed, like my back is going down into the bed and my legs are starting to rise up. I am like "wait a minute, what the hell? What is going on?" I looked to her side and I noticed that she was giggling with laugher. I said "Hey what are you doing?" at that point she was readjusting the number back to the firmness and I see myself adjusting back up to the level where I had it set for. Completely childish in my mind, I am thinking. At this point, I am like "so, why are you doing this?"

She was like "doing what?"

I said "why are you playing with the number of the firmness of my side of the bed?"

"I didn't do anything. I am going back to bed; you are disturbing my sleep" she said.

"You are pretty childish. I am starting to see that you are like a kid sometimes" I said. I am almost certain that you did move my phone that night.

She replies "really? Really …? You are going there? I see that you are argumentative. You like to argue a lot" she said.

I replied saying "no, I don't like to argue. I am calling things out that I notice about you and I see what you are doing. You are coming off as childish to me more than anything thing." She ignores me, lays down and she goes to sleep.

I mentioned this because I am beginning to see that that conversation, we had in the car coming back from our 4th of July trip about her being a handful and asking if I am sure I wanted to be with her was starting to make sense to me now. I was starting to put things together about this girl and I was seeing that she was doing things and then claiming not to be doing them. It was like she was trying to make me crazy and doubt myself, not to notice the things she was doing. I have never experienced anything like this. At this point, I am starting to be turned off by it. Again, the cycle will repeat the next morning – we get up, she goes and get breakfast, prepare everything for me. She did a really good job of damage control. While she would do these things, she would follow it up with really good acts of kindness and being a real sweetheart. That could make you overlook the things show was doing. It was like minor childish things at the time, so I didn't really take it too seriously. Nevertheless, it was still annoying and I did not realize how bad of a character that a person had to be to do these types of things. I didn't know what I was dealing with.

In the morning, I mentioned to her "what you pulled last night, you know that was really childish, right?" Yet, she denied doing anything.

"I don't know what you are talking about she said".

I laughed and said "okay, maybe you are just childish and silly" I said.
"What? Are you disrespecting me? Why would you call me childish and silly?" She said.

"Because your actions are real juvenile and silly at times; you play a lot and that's fine. But there is a time for playing and there is a time for being serious. Seems like you have a lot of unresolved issues in you that hasn't allowed you to grow up" I responded.

Her replied afterwards was just a long stare and she replied "you know what? I do need to grow at times. I don't want to talk about this now. Can we just have a good morning today?" I was like "wow... you just want to have a good morning. You didn't want to talk about this? You think this is going to iron itself out?" she didn't reply. I left it alone.

I was never the type bent on arguing anyway. I said what I had to say and I left it. Once we got back into town, I told her I wanted to spend some time on my own. At this point, she had completely gotten on my nerves.

She says "oh, you want time alone now? What is that supposed to mean".

I said "I need space like an astronaut. I want some time alone."

She says "are you trying to spend time with another bitch?"

I just told her “listen, I am not going to go there with you, I’m not going get into an argument with you.”

Now, I noticed from her that she would try to get me to engage into a confrontation with her. I was always calm and collective, but this individual is different. She wouldn’t let things rest. She would press, and press and press until you get into an argument with her. She definitely left a bad impression on me and I was starting to label her as a chick that was into playing games. In fact, I felt I had had enough and I had to tell her. “I feel like you are about playing games”, I told her.

“I am not into playing games. I want to be with you. I want something serious” she replied.

“if this is the way you act; if this how you handle things like the immature stuff you’ve been doing you that, I have called you out on, I don’t want any parts of you”, I responded.

The strangest thing that would happen after I would confront her about her behavior is that she would get to the point of coming to me to say “okay, I was just playing and sometimes I play around and I am kiddish at times but I don't mean anything by it."

"What kind of guys have you been with before that you are okay with just playing all the time? You are not a teenage girl; you are a grown woman and you are still playing these types of games. Something is definitely off." I thought to myself.

I thought I could help her through. Maybe that's not what she wants. So, I replied her: """ You know what? You goanna have to act in a totally different way if you intend to be around me and I will need you to be more mature."

She didn't argue with me; instead she replied saying "maybe I do need to mature. That's something I never thought I needed. But I am not opposed to it."

Once again I left the conversation alone. I have never dealt with any of that stuff and it didn't make any sense to me, yet I was still deeply engaged in being with her. I cannot tell you why at this point because of all that I had to tolerate. Despite this, I still decided to give her the benefit of the doubt, which I would pay for deeply later.

Interpretation

Narcissists are all about games. They just happen to throw you off. They call this crazy making. A lot of them ensure that they are disturbing your sleep or your rest in some sort of way by depriving you of sleep so you cannot properly think clearly.

Causing confusion is a strong tactic for them to be effective at manipulation. They need confusion to operate efficiently and effectively for control. If there is no confusion, you are allowed to think clearly about them and the clearer perception you have of them, the more likely you are to put things together regarding the totality of your interaction with them and how you see them. You will pass judgment quite quickly and you will move yourself out of alignment with them. The crazy making is to make you unsure. They may attempt to gaslight you as well.

Gaslighting is basically a very sinister tactic to make a person think that they are losing their mind, that what they think of about their reality isn't true. This happens because the other person would deny everything, knowing that they have done something but still deny it. So, it throws the ball back in your court to figure out whether it happened or not. A narcissist knows how to do this but balances it out with an act of kindness, gratitude and servitude towards you so that you end up forgiving them or forgetting about it. This is what they are masters of doing- creating the confusion and operating from a position of control.

Chapter 4: The Discovery

All the patience and understanding that I had with this individual so far were soon to be challenged in a real way. My questioning of her behavior was causing a major emotional reaction in her. She started becoming passive and aggressive and at times would refuse to speak or communicate at all with me. She also had to quit her job as well because she was starting to get into conflicts with her co-workers and she felt that everyone was against her. Guess who received the blame for her quitting her job? You guessed it, that's right. It was me. I got blamed for it. I was starting to get blamed for every single wrong thing going on with her.

She ended up moving back in with her mother, which she really did not want to do. She had a bad relationship with her mother and sometimes, they got into really bad arguments. Whenever that happened, she would ask to come over to spend the night with me. I would allow her to come over to give her with a bit of break from arguing with her mother. Unlike other times before, when we first met, we had fun being together. This time, she was deliberately starting arguments and conflicts with me. She would try to tell me how to put on a tie, as if she knew how to put on a tie. Of course, I would ignore her and that would agitate her. To her, I wasn't listening to her and I wasn't being affected by her either. She would go on to make rude comments like "you are not looking right with that tie on", "it looks ugly" or "it doesn't look good on you". She was nitpicking and provoking me to get a reaction out of me. I have to admit that at times, I was really annoyed with her and I wanted her ass to leave.

Whenever I told her about how she was irritating me or give her an ultimatum to leave or quit behaving in that way, she would go into the victim mode and say; "oh! I was just playing. I think you look nice actually in your little tie. I only pick on you like that because I think it's cute. You don't have to be mean to me and not want me to play around."

"So, you get a kick out of irritating me, putting me down?" I would reply.

She would just smirk and walk off. Later, she would come back with an apology and follow it up with something sweet.

Whenever I got back from work, she would already have dinner ready with the dining table decorated with candle light and then she would read a letter about how she adores me and how special I am to her. It made me feel better for the moment. Yet, it made me feel how much of an asshole I was, how ungrateful I was because I did not show enough enthusiasm about her complimenting me or reading a letter telling me how much she adores me.

It was like nothing that I had experienced before in my life. Never have I ever seen someone's mood change so rapidly on drop of a dime. She would go from being sweet, calm and loving one minute to being enraged and mean at other times. In a few hours later, she is apologizing and loving again. I knew one thing for certain and that is that I was getting fed up with this unpredictable character and mood swings that she was showing me.

I was already considering doing research on bipolar disorder because I was certain that that was what she had; and if I had to be with her, I had to deal with that. I visited a local bookstore and asked that book seller if they had any book on mental health. I was directed to the psychology section where I discovered a book on borderline and narcissist disorder. I purchased it and rushed home to read it.

As I began to browse through the pages, I started to feel helpless about what I was finding out. Page after page, I began to get confirmation about what I was experiencing with this girl that I was with and I felt sorry for her. I remember that night after I had read a large chunk of the book, I called her on the phone and I asked her to come over. I told her I wanted to share something with her. She agreed and asked me what I wanted to share with her. I did not want to tell her over the phone so I told her that she would see when she comes around. Of course, the curiosity was killing her. Once she got to my house, the look on her face was filled with excitement and anticipation for the surprise that she was expecting.

I sat her down, took out the book on narcissist and borderline and begin to read some of the parts I had highlighted. They were the parts of the book that related mostly with her behaviors. She started fidgeting and getting annoyed. She stopped me abruptly and said "I don't want to hear about this anymore."

"Why? What's wrong?" I asked.

"Because, I just don't like it. It sounds like you are talking about me" she said with irritation.
"Oh really… and why is that?" I asked.

She quickly initiated an argument by saying "You tricked me! I thought you had a good surprise for me. You are playing games with me."

"I was only trying to help you", I replied. "A lot of what you do is really weird to me and it makes me unattracted to you", I added.

"Well, I don't need any help from you. I know what I would be doing and I think it is cute like I told you before. I like when you get upset with me" she said.

"That's crazy as hell. Who would do such things and find humor or pleasure in that kind of stuff?" I questioned.

"Quinn you owe me for making me come all the way over here for nothing. Come into the room and fuck me now." She said.

I was hesitant but I went any way. The sex between her and me was amazing, unpredictable and spontaneous, but the thrill of it all was always short lived. I never felt that there was a genuine connection when we were intimate. It just felt like pure lust. It almost seems like every situation we would end up in which calls for accountability or for her being responsible or to behave in an appropriate was always diverted and turned into something sexual. At the time, it seemed like she had a high sex drive and she just enjoyed herself with me. I would soon realize that there was a lot more to it than what I was assuming and I would find out.

Interpretation

Narcissists are masters of deflecting. If they feel cornered, they would find a way to change the subject, or switch the subject or distract you from the issue at hand. They do not like being forced into an answer or being forced into admitting their mistakes. Instead, they like to brush it over with bouts of passionate sex or they would come with gifts or anything to take your mind off the issue at hand and they are masters of this. They love doing that because it makes them feel powerful and they want to be able to get away with anything and not having to answer or be accountable to their faults. This is one thing that if you over look or you allow the patronizing or the appeasement skills of the narcissist to overwhelm you, you will find yourself in a never-ending circle and it won't stop. The more they see you are receptive to this, the more they would do it. It would become harder for you after a while to resist it. In fact, you will almost program yourself to like it, enjoy it and you will look forward to it. Don't be appeased by them and their elaborate way of making up. It is only a distraction.

Chapter 5: The Devaluation

Every time there was an issue of importance to be addressed with this girl, she would start deflecting or try to cause some sort of distraction to alter the crux of the problem at hand. She was becoming more and more unruly by the day. It seemed like I had struck a nerve in her or cornered her the wrong way by trying to figure out what was wrong with her. I thought I knew her, but I was starting to realize that I was wrong in my assessment of her character. The devaluation phase had begun and I was torn down emotionally. One part of me felt sorry for her and had real feelings for her, but the other part of me was like there was no reason for me to still be involved with this unstable and unpredictable girl. I had enough red flags to let me go at the time; yet, I stayed. It was as if I was under some kind of spell and I couldn't just reject her or leave her.

I recalled times where she would see me frustrated from her unruly and out-of-control ways and she would say: "I am sorry baby. I didn't know that my behavior was affecting you in that kind of way. I will try to stop." Of course, all these words were in vain as their effects were very short lived. In fact, her behaviors would become worse. The more I tried to create peace and harmony, the more she would go about aggravating things and provoking me. She would call me names like "asshole and prick" for no reason. Well, she would do that just because she felt like it, especially if I wasn't complying with her demands which were usually outrageous.

I noticed how more critical she became about my choice of style or how I would eat or the time I should wake up in the morning. She started complaining about everything. It was as though she liked nothing about me now, which was confusing because in the beginning I was this perfect guy. She liked everything, but now she is filled with disgust towards me.

We were approaching the seventh month mark of us dating and the lease for where I was staying was about to be up. I asked her if she wanted to move in with me since she had already been staying over at my place.

Her response was "I don't know. I don't think I could live with someone like you. You are not up to my standard" she said.

"Wow… what? Are you trying to insult me? What the hell did you mean by that? I am not up to your standards? Oh but I was up to your standards to come over and eat my food and lay your head down whenever your mother was at your neck? But now I am not up to your standards?" I asked furiously.

"There are certain things that you do that I just don't like", She replied.

"You know what? Never mind! I have changed my mind. Go back to your mother's house. I think you will be better off staying with her anyway" I said with gross irritation.

She quickly responded "I was just playing. Jeez… you don't have to be so serious. I told you about that."

"What the hell does that mean that you are just playing? You always do this and then try to flip it. You know what? You are full of shit", I replied.

"I will move in with you. How much would I have to pay?" she said.

"It's half of course", I said.

"Half? For this place? No, I don't know about that. I would have picked a better place than this" she responded.

I turned to her and said "why does everything have to be a competition with you? Why does it always have to be a me versus you situation?"

She replied "I know what I am doing."

"Well, that doesn't reflect in your track record."

She then turned to me and said "why are you so abusive to me?

You are always putting me down."

"Whatever", I said.

While we were going back and forth in our exchange of words, I could not help but see the very words that I had been reading in the book that I bought on personality disorders. The way she was acting was lining up perfectly with all of it. I said to myself that I would start ignoring her when she starts going off with the nonsense and I would see how that works.

The book on personality disorders mentioned that narcissists don't like to be challenged and can become very defensive and hypersensitive. They use a lot of projecting and deflecting to offset this. I was starting to gain understanding I thought, until one day when I was at work. I got a text from her saying "Hey! I found a nice place that we can move to and it would be perfect for me. I can start my own daycare. It's 1800 dollars a month."
"What? 1800 a month? That's way out of the budget range I was looking to pay monthly", I texted back.

"Didn't I tell you I was going to be starting my day care?" She replied.

"Yes, but that's not in effect yet" I further replied.

"I will have clients in the first month of us moving in she said.

I would be able to cover my half."

"Are you sure about this?" I asked.

She said "Yes, I am positive."

"Okay, let's do this then", I texted back conceding to her request.

I can recall really not wanting to make the move with her. It seemed right, yet it didn't seem practical. It felt like I was probably getting myself into something I would not like later down the line. I was also considering how tough the first month would be since I would spend the bulk of the money for us to make this move. She didn't have a job at that time. On the day of the move, I had an uneasy feeling. I felt like I should have stopped while I had the chance to.

First week into our new place, she started saying that she wanted a dog and that it would help calm her anxiety.

"That's cool as long as you are willing to pay the additional three hundred dollars for the pet fee" I said.

"Why should I pay the fee when I can just keep the dog out of sight so that no one knows", She responded.

"I don't think it is a good idea. I think you should just focus on the business and the day care. You are just adding extra responsibilities that could take you away from what you are trying to do in your business.", I said.

"Plus, you don't want to get in over your head with watching kids from clients that you are seeking" I added.

"Oh my God! You never support me. You are always putting me down and doubting me", She said. I just looked at her and shook my head. She stormed off upset.

Three days later, on returning from work, I was greeted by "Hey babe" and the excitement of a small sized black curly haired dog jumping up and down on me. "Isn't it cute?" she asked.

"When did you get this dog?" I asked.

"I got him from the dog animal rescue" she replied.
"Okay, did you pay the extra pet fee?" I asked again.

"Yeah, I paid it. Don't worry about it I gave them a 300 dollar money order", she said.

Two whole months had passed after that and we had our first maintenance issue with our hot water heater leaking. Water had leaked all the way from there into the living room and passed into the kitchen. She was furious because her day care area was saturated. It was causing her to have to make adjustments which she didn't want to do. It was really cramping her style. She called maintenance, but they couldn't do very much but bring a floor fan to dry the floor and the carpet. Since it was the weekend anyway, they would have to come back during the week to get any type of work done. The earliest that would happen would be a Tuesday, but that day was a Saturday.

When Tuesday arrived, I got a call from her saying that it was important. I asked what the problem was. "The maintenance man is here and he is telling me that he can't fix it till at least one more day, because he needs a fixture that can go with the water heater for the installment and it hasn't arrived yet", she said.

"Okay, is that the earliest that they can get it fixed?" I asked. "Yes", she responded.

"Then we will have to wait for another day" I said. "I cannot stand the sorry ass maintenance crew that they have here. They are all a bunch of lazy sorry pieces of shit." She barked.

Mind you, the maintenance crew was standing right there by her side when she is saying all these disrespectful things. I told her that we would talk about it once I got home; then she ended the call.

After I left work, and upon approaching our apartment door, there was a letter folded in half and taped to the door. I grabbed it, went inside and settled to read it. It was a letter from the leasing office saying that we were in violation of the lease agreement by having a pet and not paying a pet fee. I sighed, shook my head and called her to read the letter. She started reading the letter with a look of concern on her face.

"The maintenance man probably dropped a dime on you for being disrespectful. They know who can and who is not supposed to have pets on the grounds of these apartments. And you were still talking a lot of shit to him and that possibly upset him and he went back and reported that you had a pet. Now, I suggest you go down to the leasing office and try to make that right, if it is not too late. I told you getting that dog was a bad idea." I said

As she was getting dressed to go to the leasing office, I remembered that I recalled her saying she would take care of the pet fee and pay it, but obviously she did no such thing. So, she must have lied. When she returned from the leasing office, she came back looking sad and down, and she said to me "we have to move. I talked with the property manager and I cursed her ass out."

"What the hell would you do that for", I asked. She was just looking at me with some dumbfounded look on her face. She shrugged her shoulders and said "I don't know why".
We hadn't even spent a year in that place. It's been only three months and we have to move.

Interpretation

Because narcissist behavior is so unruly and so unpredictable and it lacks impulse control, often times, they end up doing things that will either put them or the people around them in jeopardy. They don't exercise proper judgment, they don't think things through, they don't rationalize things; they just want to have what they want, regardless of the consequences. This is something that a lot of people may have found in their interaction with narcissists. You may think that you have reached an agreement with them and you are on the same page, but they are doing something totally different behind the scenes. They will tell you what you want to hear but they are going to do what they want to do at the end of the day. They can even put in you in dire situations which you have no control over from their reckless behaviors and actions. Never put your faith or trust in these individuals.

Chapter 6: The Discard: Escaping the Madness

With a three-day notice to surrender the property, we are now stuck in the situation where we have to move out and I am completely burdened by it. I took it upon myself to go to the property manager to speak to them about possible options. I was explaining to her that I couldn't afford to let this happen right now. I knew that we were not supposed to have a dog, but I assured her that we will get rid of the dog and that it would not happen again. She looked at her computer screen intensely for some seconds and said; "okay, I will redact the notice, only on the account that you are coming to me with respect like an adult. As for your girlfriend, you sir have a serious problem on your hands."

I nodded my head in agreement and said "I am finding that out myself".

I went back to my apartment and saw the narcissist packing and I told her "Hey look! I have something to tell you. I managed to get the property manager to give us a second chance, so that we don't have to get evicted."

She said "so, you went down there kissing her ass?"

"Stop your shit. You should be thankful that we still have a place to live" I said.

"Whatever Quinn" she responded.

At this point I was feeling like I had an ungrateful, spoilt human on my hand that was going to end up bringing me down. I started to use the tips that I had learnt from the book I bought about borderline personality and narcissist. I started grey-rocking her. This method basically makes you become boring and not quite interesting to a narcissist. Ignoring her fights and being something that is not engaging to them. She could feel the difference in how I was acting towards her. She said "you don't want me anymore. Do you?"

"Yeah, I do. I am good. We are just working things out", I responded.

"No, you are not. You are just trying to buy time to leave me" she said

Even though she was absolutely right, I warded off her words as though she was completely wrong, but in reality, I had enough of her. This girl was causing my life to flip upside down. It was one thing after the other. It felt like I was living inside a fun house. She started increasing arguments with me and that became her daily dose of making me uncomfortable. I felt like a prisoner in my own home and I felt trapped as well. I was stuck in a lease with a deranged lunatic and something had to be done.

One major turning point in our situation was a time when she went into the store and took her client's baby that she was babysitting with her. On the way back home, the father of the baby was en route to the house as well and they arrived at the house at the same time. I was going outside to the car to help with groceries bags. The baby's father was opening the rear passenger door to get his child out of the car and all I remember was hearing him yelling really loud saying "why the hell is my child not buckled up in the car seat? Are you fucking serious? You just put my child in without properly ensuring his safety? I am done with you. I am letting my wife know that we are done with you as well."

She said nothing as he was ripping her new asshole. All I could do was to stand by and watch because he was totally justified to be acting the way he was. The loss of this client meant no income for her. She would have to start all over looking for a new client so that she can have a new income coming in. The fact that we lived in an area that was not easy to get to was a huge problem for her. It was fairly far out and was inconvenient to people in the highway communities. A lot of parents that did inquire about her and her daycare services and rarely followed up once they found out where her location was. This left me having to pay all the bills without any help from her. I was quickly growing to dislike her and wanting to get away from her as quick as possible.

I started putting an exit strategy together. Finances were limited as I was the only one with the source of income at the time. I truly believed that she had a supernatural six sense of some type that somehow gave her insight into what I might be planning or thinking. I remember one time in the morning while I was eating breakfast and preparing to go to work, she walked past me by the table, bent over like she was about to pick something and knocked over my coffee, spilling it on my pants and shirt. She hurriedly apologized and made it seem like it was an accident, but I knew better. She did that on purpose. The motion of her arm was too deliberate and she pulled her hand back from reaching across the table. She forced her hands outward to knock over my coffee which spilled on me. Another argument ensued and now I am going to be late for work because of it.

Getting back home on that day, I decided that enough was enough. It was time to leave; I didn't know where I was going, but it was time to get the hell away from her. All I knew was that at this point, she was undoubtedly a narcissist. I started to put together a plan that would allow me to leave the situation without her knowing what I was up to. I could feel the tension in the air between us. She started to increase the level of her disrespect towards me. Usually when I would get home from work, she would be waiting up for me with my food ready that she had prepared. Now, there was no food prepared and she would be in the room closed off; not even coming out to acknowledge me. Although, I understood that she knew that her time with me was quickly coming to an end. The more I ignored her passive aggression, the more she would be irritated. Having me around as her source of supply was nearing quickly.

She started to counter by initiating the breakup. Out of nowhere one day, she said she has a guy coming over to help her with her day care transportation. Now she never told me anything about this before until the day she had to interview him. Of course, this was supposed to be done while I was at work. I said to myself "okay… I see what's going on here. She is looking for a new source to fill in my place and possibly make me jealous to make me think about staying, but I wasn't going for it".

I told her "that's fine, do what you have to do."

She said "hmm…I will please believe that boo."

At this time, I knew she would be trying to get a major rise out of me that can make me react to what she was doing. But boy was it hard and I was holding back from reacting. I really wanted to tell her off and let her know I see what she was doing to me but I held myself back. You see, narcissists are very good at getting people out of character. They have various methods of provoking you to anger. I knew that it was only a matter of time until this situation spilled over into something more serious to where she may start to invoke physical violence next.

She was pissed off having to witness her control of me and the situation we were in slip out of her grasp. When I got back home that evening, she was all made up dressed pretty sexually in my opinion, with suggestive clothes on. She had a tight white and black dress; her hair was done up and her makeup was on. I said "you look nice. What's the special occasion?"

"Nothing, I told you I had someone was coming over earlier, and I was going to be interviewing him to be a driver for my day care service" she said.

"Okay… you want him to see that he would be getting a total package while working for you perhaps," I said with a chuckle.

"Yupp… I sure did", she responded

"I got you", I said.

The writing was on the wall for me and I decided that night that I was done. I began putting plans together that would involve me moving out of the state we were in to an entirely different state. I wasn't exactly sure how it was going to work out but I knew I had to get out of there. The plan took about a week to be carried out. I needed to get my last pay check and give a notice of separation from my job. In the meantime, I was spending as much time away from home as I could and I wanted to minimize my contact with her as much as possible. I also was packing the things I needed into the small SUV that I had at the time which was a "ford explore". I had a decent amount of room in there to get as many things as I could to take with me. I couldn't move everything at once because it would draw attention to what I was doing and possibly give my pan away.

In about two weeks, the rent for the next month was coming up and I had zero intentions on paying. One day after I had finished taking the shower, she came to me and said "I changed my mind about getting someone to help me with my daycare. I can't just trust anyone like that to work with when I don't even know them. Even after interviewing him, I don't feel comfortable about him."

"Yeah that is good. You can't predict how that would work out", I said to her

Deep down, I could care less about what she was doing or what she had decided at the time. It was over for me and my mind was completely made up. She said "I am going to look for more clients and just try to make this daycare thing work out. I am tired of being this broke and shit." It was nearing the end of the week and she had an interview set up for a possible client that Friday afternoon. She was going to meet them at an agreed place though, which was their house. I remember thinking to myself that I can make my exit then while she is gone.

I know you may wonder why I wanted to leave in that way at least; I will explain. If you are dealing with a narcissist or someone mentally unstable the last thing that you want to present is an abandonment situation where you are leaving them for good. It will not end well and you are more than likely to end up with a domestic violence situation on your hands. If that happens, you won't be going anywhere but the local county jail in cuffs. With that being said, I waited for her to leave for her interview. I collected the rest of my things and I left. I set the address into my GPS and off I went.

Interpretation

Narcissists know what they are doing. In fact, this is not their first time of doing that to someone else. They know the cues of when someone is tired of them. They know when someone is possibly ready to leave them alone. Sometimes, they would initiate arguments, fights that may even be physical. All to say that they are in control, because every narcissist is a control freak. They have to be in control of everything around them, therefore if you are trying to escape from them, they feel they are out of control and it is not a good feeling for them. To break you down mentally, they start to target you, pick at you, insult you and make you as uncomfortable as possible. This is mainly to wear your mind down so that you are too weighed down and dejected to make a clear decision that would be in your benefit. It is important to never allow them to know what you are doing or how you are really feeling. They would use this to better position themselves to stop you from what you want to do or target you in a different way another time. When you decide, keep everything normal. Don't give them any inclination that something is wrong and make your exit like a thief in the night. If a narcissist knows what you are doing, they will try everything possible to try to disrupt your plan, especially when the narcissist is ready to go all out. They have no mercy, they have not a care and a lot of time, people get hurt a lot of times. Just be careful if you are witnessing this type of behavior.

Chapter 7: Moving on From the Narcissist

With all my belongings packed and a full tank of gas, I set out to Denver. I wasn't exactly sure what I was going to do once I got there, but I did have my mother if things go too bad. Though my mother wouldn't have mind, I was not trying to make myself a burden by choosing that option. I was a grown man now, and my mindset was "if my mother wasn't here, what would I do?" That mentality put me in a state of mind of pure self-reliance and survival, and I chose not to use my mother as a backup. It was midsummer and the cold wasn't going to be an immediate factor for me to worry about just yet. But it did cause concerns because Denver's weather can be brutal.

Two hours into my drive, I get a message from the narcissist saying "where are you? I need to get money to go to the store and get some things and I need to borrow thirty dollars for some hair stuff that I need to get." I texted her back and said "I am gone."

"Duurrh… obviously you are gone because you are at work, but I am talking about when you will get back home", she replied.

"I am gone for good. It's over and I am not coming back" I texted back.
She then called me on the phone and when I answered she said "what the hell are you talking about?"

I said "exactly what I told you in the text message. It's over and I am done."
"I don't understand. What do you mean you are done? Stop playing around. I am serious. I need to go to the store and I need to borrow 30 dollars", she said, almost not believing her ears.

I told her that "I am not playing any game. I am done with all of your shit. I told you one day you were going to look for me and I would be gone. I don't want anything to do with you anymore. We are finished for good. Bye" I told her, and then I ended the call.

She then proceeded to continuously call my phone for over a dozen times form back to back. She then texted "oh... I see. You have another bitch. Well, we shall see who shall have the last laugh. Nigga!" I still kept ignoring her and finally after 10 minutes of calling and texting she stopped trying to get a hold of me.

I can remember while driving I was thinking to myself "I am free at last". It felt like I had escaped off a slave plantation. An over whelming sense of peace started to come over me and as I was driving down the highway headed as far away from her ass as I could. Literally, it felt like a big weight had been lifted off my shoulders. So many thoughts were still racing through my mind at that time. It hit me about nine hours into my fifteen-hour drive to Denver that "wow... this is reality. It is over."

Then I would switch back to "but man do I feel sorry for her because with the way that she was and how she carried on being reckless and crazy with her behavior, she is bound to run into some rough patches and really go down in life in a major way. Leaving her and without me supporting her would put her in a pretty bad situation. But I could not take being around her anymore. It was starting to affect my mental health. I was starting to get high blood pressure and migraines and heavy amounts of stress due to constant arguments and negativity coming from her. Driving on the highway, all of a sudden began to feel lonely as night time began to approach. While I was headed to the direction of the sun setting, I noticed myself getting sleepy. I pulled into a tuck stop to grab a few snacks and wet my face to try to keep myself refreshed to stay awake.

As I was walking back to my car, I saw another message from the narcissist saying "okay, I am sorry for acting out the way that I did. I didn't know that my behaviors were affecting you that much and I overreacted in a lot of situations that had nothing to do with you. Now please forgive me and come back home." Normally, that would have been enough to lure me right back in because I wanted to believe that she actually meant what she was saying and was really trying to make amends and right her wrong. But too many times when I fell for this and we got back together, everything would be great for about a week and then the same shit that she did before and apologized for, she did all over again. All the things that she said that she would not do, she ended up doing them again. I was on to her game of trying to appease me to get me to be back with her, and then too many times she would switch back up in a matter of days or weeks. I had zero belief in her now, and I was not buying into her lies anymore. I ignored the text messages and proceeded on my way to Denver.

I arrived in Denver in the early hours of the morning, tired as hell. I started looking out for cheap motels on my phone to stay in for a while till I could find another job to get back on my feet. Spending the majority of the money from my pay check to get into a hotel room would leave me just flat broke with no money. Yet, I needed to have something that could hold me over till I could transition into something more permanent. I managed to find a pretty decent hotel that wasn't too expensive. After all, I only had one thousand three hundred dollars from my pay check. The room I got was about nine hundred and fifty dollars for the monthly option. I booked it and went to a small diner to get some breakfast until the 11 am check in.

As I was eating, I got a call from the narcissist. This time, I answered and was greeted with a much calmer voice. She said "Good morning. What are you doing? Where are you at? Are you at some girl's house?"

"No, I told you before. We are done. We are over. I have already left the state." I said.

"No! Why? Why would you do that? That's fucked up. Are you serious? How long are you gone for ", she asked

I replied saying "For good, it's over. How many times do I have to say it?"

"Fuck you! I have been tired of your ass anyway. By the way, here is something for your sorry ass to look at", she replied. She then sent me a message of a picture with her and a guy hugging from a selfie she took. She said "there you see that? You can ever make me that happy."
I just hung the phone on her ending the call. I did not even bother to respond. Then she texted me again and said "you aren't shit and never going to be shit. You were nothing to lose anyway. Goodbye and good riddance."

This shit was really going in on me. She was trying to crush me emotionally. I am not going to lie; those words did hurt, especially when I really loved her and cared about her. Man, it was hard hearing that, but at the same time, it was bringing a revelation to me about how fake and phony she was as a person and that I wasn't wrong about her what I thought about her from reading all that information about personality disorder.

When I checked in my room that morning, the first thing I did was to take a long shower. That hot water felt so good running down my face. After the shower, I passed out and slept for about good twelve hours straight. When I woke up, I felt refreshed, but still feeling a little drained. I was thinking about what the narcissist had said to me. It was on that day that I decided to exercise that energy and heartbroken emotions that I was feeling.

I decided to create a YouTube channel and my decision was to talk about narcissists based on my experience from dealing with one. I felt that it would be a way for me to heal myself by sharing my knowledge of what I went through with people. After creating my YouTube channel, the very first morning, I posted my first video called "My experience with a narcissist". I was a nervous, but I mustered courage and spoke from the heart. It felt good to let some steam off my chest by sharing my experience publicly.

Every day, I would go out job hunting and interviewing. Sometimes, I would park my car and record videos of my experience with the narcissist. Then, I would upload it on YouTube. I started to get out the information. As I did more videos, it became easier and easier. My subscribers were increasing as well. I was starting to like this YouTube thing as it was becoming my unorthodox method of self therapy. I always felt a little bit better after I recorded a video. I still had this feeling of bewilderment within me, because even though I had read the book on borderline disorders and narcissist, I still felt the effect of cognitive dissonance upon me.

I just could not believe that someone could be so disruptive, cold-hearted and fake or pretending to love and care for you. For a period of time the whole cognitive dissonance thing was what I wrestled with the most. I researched more on the subject and studied for as much as I could. I was learning about what the after effects from being with a narcissist entailed and also to add to my understanding of a narcissist personality in general. It would also help me to be more effective in spreading knowledge on my YouTube channel. The more I took in about narcissists' personality disorder, the more I became comfortable about my decision to leave the narcissist and never to return back.

I only had thirty days at the hotel that I was staying at and still hadn't landed a job yet. Meanwhile, I was starting to get emails from the narcissist, this time with more hovering attempts to get me to come back. This time she was apologizing for sending that picture and how she talking bad about me and other foul things that she said. She stated that she didn't know how much I really cared for her but she was angry being the reasons to why she did the things that she did. She made it sound so sincere that time. I thought about it for a second, like maybe she really is sorry about what she has done or maybe she is just acting up like other times because she couldn't express herself properly. She asked me to unblock her that she wanted to talk to me and that it was really urgent for her to speak with me.

I went against my better judgment and all the information that I knew about breaking the no-contact rule. I reached out and called her. She answered and said "why are you doing this? Why aren't you coming back? I am sorry about everything. Don't be mad at me."

I said "I don't believe you and besides all of the disrespectful shit you said to me, I am good."

"So, you are not coming back?" She asked

"No, absolutely not", I replied

"It's fine. That is why I have been fucking the neighbor while you were working all this time. You aren't shit like I said and can stay gone. I don't even care anymore. I am cool on your ass." She said

I hung up ending the call yet again. This time I kicked myself in the ass. Every time I answer this girl, she goes in on me with the most disrespectful shit that a person should not say to someone who they supposedly love, proving that she never gave two fucks about me anyway in the first place. She was trying to emotionally destroy me and leave me as messed up in the head as she possibly could. It was at this moment that I had an epiphany. It was time to block all forms of connections that she could use to get to me. I went no contact to the extreme and this time I changed my phone number and email so that she had no way of contacting me.

This would be my final decision in moving forward and to not allow myself to be tempted or drawn back in or to speak with her again.

Interpretation

Moving on from a toxic relationship with someone that you thought cared about you is never easy. Many times, we are confused and left without closure. Sometimes, we develop weird unexplainable fixations to those who have mistreated us. When this happens, we have developed a trauma bond to that person which most causes us grief and distrust in some way. Our letting go can be seen as quitting or not being good enough as we criticize ourselves to knowing. We tend to ask: Why us? Why did we seem to find ourselves in this situation? Even more so unhealthy is when those who cannot recognize abuse and choose to stay put in unhealthy situations become permanently damaged, not being able to recognize normalcy. They get programmed to accept and stay in unhealthy situations over and over again. Whenever your mind feels weary and worn down, or when the feeling of sadness overwhelms you, ask yourself this: “Is anything you are currently dealing with worth it? Is it adding any value to your life? Is it making you a better person? If your answer is no, then you should leave immediately, because what’s there is never going to be for you.

Chapter8: My Transition After Leaving the Narcissist

Now that I had finally caught off all forms of communication with the narcissist, the challenge to myself was to keep it that way. I was motivated more than ever to bounce back on my feet from the crushing defeat that I took from dealing with the narcissist. I was filled with anger from a bruised ego, to not only redeem myself but to reach a level of success in my life which I had never reached before. My YouTube channel would become somewhat of a diary of all that happened to me while I was with the narcissist. It seemed like every week, the number of subscribers to my channel had been doubling. I was excited and uplifted with even more confidence that I will do my best being a Youtuber.

Meanwhile, back at hotel, I was running out of days and I did not have enough money to pay for a full month stay again. Even more so, if I kept paying the rent at the hotel without having any option to move forward, I will only be wasting money. Yet, if I tried to play catch up to get money to move out of the hotel, that would be like a trapped situation to me. I made up my mind that I would sleep in my car and save money until I had enough to rent my own apartment. As the days went by, I started to pack my things to mentally prepare myself for living out in my car for at least another month.

The monetization from my YouTube videos was starting to add up. I remember my first payment being just a little under two hundred dollars. I mainly use that money for gas, to pay my membership at the gym, while the rest was spent on food, soap and stuffs like that. It was going to be quite an adjustment but as it stood; I had no other choice. Those last few days at the hotel came to an end fast. I remember this warehouse development that had just been built but not occupied when I went out looking for a job. The location was pretty far from anything residential. The only other thing near it was a cemetery that was adjacent to it. It was fairly safe and peaceful so I decided that I would just use that location temporarily.

Over the next thirty-six days, this would be home (if that's what you want to call it). I would work certain available jobs that I could find on days that they had jobs to keep the cash flow coming in. It would usually be odd jobs like construction clean up, packing or cleaning. At night, when it was time to turn in, I would go to the twenty-four-hour gym that I had a membership at and work out for a little while before I go back to my spot. I would park close to a large wall that was next to a dumpster in between the loading dock in the building. It wasn't great, but it gave me a little more privacy.

A lot of times, I would go to the truck stop store to eat as they had a pretty good diner and decent food there. If that wasn't an option, then it was a sausage or ravioli.

Sleeping in the car being a 6 ft. 5 inches was definitely a challenge even though it was a nice size SUV and I was able to lay the seat from the back all the way down to make myself a make shift bed. Despite doing this, it was till uncomfortable. I cannot tell you how many times in the morning when I was up how sore my back was or how stiff my neck was for sleeping in the most uncomfortable position. After a week of this, I had already had enough to force myself to go through it. My mother would call me to ask me what I was up to and how I was. I would always say "I am good Mom; everything is cool". It was like she could tell that something was wrong and that there was more to it than I was saying. But I didn't want to tell my mother what I was really going through. I didn't want to have her worry about me, nor did I want to have her rescue me. All she knew from what I had told her was that I moved and I had a friend that I was staying by. Another part of me felt embarrassed and like a failure for allowing myself to go through what I had gone through only to land flat on my ass and fall rock bottom. I don't know, I guess it was the pride in me that did not want to seem helpless and pitiful. I kept a lot that I was going through from pretty much all of my family and anyone else that I knew.

This shit was embarrassing to me. All I knew as that I had to keep grinding and there was no turning back. I just had to keep my faith up and trust in the Lord that he will keep seeing me through what I was going through. I recall one of the days when I returned to my spot at the warehouse; I looked up at the stars t saying to myself "never again will I be in this position. Never again!" So many thoughts ran through my head on why the hell I did not just leave the narcissist girl alone the very first time that she pulled some shady stuff on me. Now, look at me sitting out here in my car by an unoccupied warehouse. This can't be how life is meant to be. I couldn't allow myself to dwell on the "should have" or "could have" for too long. That wasn't going to do me any good now considering the position that I was in. Rather, I kept making videos for my YouTube channel.

In my mind I was thinking that if I kept the pace up by putting the videos up on a consistent level that I was putting them at, I would have a very serious amount paid out from YouTube the next month which I seriously needed. It would help me tremendously. As my popularity started to rise on YouTube, I started to get emails from my viewers enquiring booking one on one consultation with me. I wasn't prepared at the moment because I was not expecting people to be reaching out to me for advice. Also, I was new to this YouTube thing and I was still finding my way with the new channel that I just started. Shit! I didn't even have a consultation rate for that matter.

I winged it initially and just charged a small fee for my first few clients. It was like God knew what I needed because these clients booking appointments with I was starting to give me light at the end of the tunnel. I was starting to have a boost in my morale. I guess the floodgates of blessings were opening. I got an offer from a young lady in Germany to design me a website for free. She said she was grateful for the knowledge that I had been putting out on my channel. She added that she noticed that I didn't have anything giving more information about me like a bio or anything like that and it would be certainly a benefit for me if I did.

"No, I don't have a website currently. Indeed, I would be honored if you help me with one", I replied.
"No problem, I would need you to send me your bio and any other specific information that you would want to see up there", she requested.

I obliged and did just that. I also included my consultation and fees. Having a website was going to make things better and smoother for me. About a week later, as promised, she emailed me saying "you are going to need a domain and host". I paid the money to her to have her set up, and so that she could put up to make my website visible.

"Here you go, I hope you like it" she said.

"Thank you" I said. Wow… Look at God"

Finally, I have a website with all of my information and services that I could now pass on to my subscribers. I put it to use immediately. On the very next video that I posted, I mentioned it. The consultation requests started coming in and before I knew it, I was booking consultations left and right. At the rate that I was going, I wouldn't have to be sleeping in my car for too long.

Interpretation

When we are faced with having to leave something behind or cutting something off, which may not be good for us, one of our biggest challenges is overcoming the fear of moving on and transitioning to the unknown. A lot of times, we get too complacent and familiar with what is known to us and we grow an unbreakable attachment towards it. We stay because we have developed and understood that system that we are in and may become too comfortable in it. The sheer thought of letting go and moving on outside of that can strike us with fear.

We sometimes never push ourselves to our fullest potentials because we are too preoccupied with being where we are. It is better to make a move even though you may not have a full plan. It is better to do something than to stay stuck. Always push yourself, challenge yourself. Never be afraid to let go and let God.

Chapter 9: The Starting Point/Starting to See Progress

Now that I was getting more one on one consultations, it gave me a boost in confidence that I would be getting out of my situation just as I had planned. I gave myself thirty days to move out of my car and in to a permanent location. At the rate I was going through with my consultations, I was sure that I could do just what I had planned. My YouTube channel was doing well and the comments that I received were encouraging me. I realized that a lot of people had begun to take notice of the information that I was sharing in my videos. The most important thing that I noticed them saying was about me was how accurate I was and how the information resonated deeply with them.

They said it was almost as if I were talking to them pers onally. That was a good thing for me at the time, becaus e it made me feel that I was being effective in deliverin g the information in such a way that people could find it relatable. I was glad they could make the
most of the information I was giving.

There was one significant instance that stood out to me at this particular time that had a major impact on me, and that was when I received an email from Dr. Griffin, a behavioralist. He specializes in dealing with personality disorders and other psychological deficiencies that people may have. He had a question about a demonic look that narcissists give and wanted to get my point of view on that. At that time, I remember telling him that I wasn't too familiar with it and I could not tell if I had experienced it or not when I was dealing with the narcissist, I never connected a demonic look to her when she was angry. He then told me about his own experience; he shared what he noticed and what he had seen from narcissists when they get angry and the demonic look that upon their faces. He then asked if I'd ask my audience if they'd been familiar with that look, or if they'd seen that look before. It was just a matter of getting an open opinion from my YouTube audience. I promised to make a video of it, and would follow up on it at a later time. He agreed, and that was the end of the conversation.

I made a move to reach out to him after I made a video asking if people saw that demonic face on their narcissist when they were dealing with them or in a relationship with them. A lot of people said from their responses that they had experienced see the demonic look and that they had gone through a similar experience. I remember emailing Dr. Griffin telling him that people responded well to the video that I made about the question he had asked about the look that narcissists make when they are angry, which may appear demonic at times. I gave him a rundown of the replies I got from what people were saying. He told me that he was watching the video as well and that it was interesting to see how many people had experienced it. He said that it was something that he was always wondering about. He then went on to say that he was quite impressed with the way I analyzed and brought forth the message in a way that he was able to understand and feel comfortable with. He added that I did a very good job of explaining this disorder in such a way that the average person who had no knowledge of narcissistic personality disorder would be able to identify the features of the disorder based on how I presented the information. That was really great to me, because it made me feel like I really had a gift, I really had a special talent for this, and I had a deep understanding of the disorder, from my own personal experience. It was huge for the doctor to recognize this and give me that acknowledgement. He told me that he wanted me to talk to a young lady who was trying to get hold of me. He made it known that he had spoken to her and she mentioned that she follows me and she wanted to speak with me. He said she was into filmmaking and podcast and it would be a good idea if we linked up. At the time, I had a lot of stuffs going on and I wasn't necessarily interested initially because I was just starting to get my feet in the door with the whole YouTube thing. I hadn't really gotten a full grasp of that yet and people were just starting to come to me with a lot of things that they wanted to collaborate on with me. It was pretty overwhelming. All I was really concerned about was getting out of the situation I was in. I had dug a hole for myself with getting involved with the narcissist. The vision I was trying to keep consistent with was to get an apartment, something more than being on the street and sleeping in my car. That was the most important thing to me.

I needed to make as much money as I could at that time to recover from the losses that had already occurred, and that would mean that I needed some other type of passive income. I came up with an idea and developed an e-course in audio format that would give a comprehensive overview of what narcissists do in certain given situations. The premise of the e-course was to give a breakdown on narcissistic jargons, the tactics and the things people should be looking out for to avoid being a victim of narcissists. It took me about thirty days to complete the e-course audio and I would put aside twenty minutes a day no matter what to work on different sections of the e-course. My plan was that, once the e-course had been completed, I would go ahead and sell it to my audience, my subscribers, and use that revenue to launch other projects. I had to find a place to stay before this would come in to play though. So, I started looking hard for a place to stay and once I had enough to at least put a deposit down on an apartment I could get into, specifically a one bedroom. I found one that was pretty basic, like entry level, and rented it for one thousand and two hundred dollars a month. They had a special going on where I could move in with only two hundred dollars as deposit, and a hundred dollars for the application fee.

So, I went through the process and basically waited. They told me it would take about three days before they got the background check and all the other related checks to be cleared, after which I would be called and given an answer. I was praying like hell that everything was going to work smoothly and I could move in as soon as possible. I managed to save up enough money between the consultations that I was doing to get the amount I needed.

One of the sweet deals about this particular place was that they were offering a free first month, which was exactly what I needed, and it was one of the main reasons why I chose that place. I'd need at least three hundred dollars to move in, plus other things like renter insurance and other things I'd need. But that would be good enough for me at that time if I didn't have to pay for the first month of rent. I will never forget the day the leasing agent form that apartment community called me and said "Hey Quinn, good news! Everything checked out, you can move in. When you get here, we will need your security deposit and you can come get your keys". Man, I was so happy and overwhelmed with joy because after living in my car for the past thirty something days, it was a relief to know that I was going to be in my own place. I no longer have to stay outside living in my car, nor will I be exposed to the elements being uncomfortable as hell.

I drove so fast down to the leasing office that one would think I was shot out of a rocket. All I could think of was that I was finally off the street. I didn't have to live in my car anymore. Now, all I need to do was focus on my channel as a YouTuber and post better content. I signed the lease, picked up my keys and moved into my apartment. The first thing I did, of course, was to thank God and reflect for at least ten to fifteen minutes. "Wow! I am so glad to have this" I exclaimed when I got in. We take some things for granted, like where we stay, but when you have to resort to more extremes of having to live in your car or being homeless at some point, it will humble you. It will make you realize that even when you may not have the best, anything is better than being out in the streets. That's what I was thinking at the time when I was sitting in my new apartment. I've just been reflective and thankful about everything that I went through up to this point.

At this point, my mentality and the surge of energy that I had after reflecting was that I had to hit it and hit it hard. With about one thousand and two hundred dollars to pay for the rent and a note to pay for the car, I had to get on with it. I've had to keep doing more and more. Right now, I couldn't stop. I wasn't working on a regular job now, so there was no one to help me or bail me out if things got rough.

Once I completed the audio recordings for the e-course, I introduced it to my YouTube audience. It started to sell pretty good as well. On top of that, I was still doing really well with my consultations. They were still coming in consistently, on a daily basis for that fact. Now, my financial situation on the other hand was starting to put me in a position to do more in regards to putting other business ventures together. I was starting to be less worried about my chances of making it being a YouTuber full time without having to get any other job to make money.

Two things that dawned upon me, which became a revelation of the truth, were perseverance and courage. Those two things were what got me through some of the toughest times after I left the narcissist. It was difficult to have to limit myself to certain things that I wasn't used to, having sleep in my car and not having a job. Once I became a YouTuber, I didn't have that kind of security anymore, because I was an entrepreneur now. I've had to make a way for myself. Even more so, it was all dependent on me, whether I ate or starved.
It takes courage to jump out on a limb like that like and trust that you can make it happen on your own.

I wasn't in any way out of the woods just yet, because I had taken on another responsibility to rent an apartment that I had been renting for a whole year, and I had to keep it going. I had to be consistent and diligent in my work

in order to maintain it. I had to be creative and efficient at what I was trying to produce, so that I could keep up with the momentum of this new success. For me, there was no turning back; failure was not an option. And I had a chip on my shoulders to be honest with you.
I had a chip because the narcissists told me a lot of nasty and unpleasant things about myself when I left. One day, I told her I was going to be a life coach. She said, "I don't know why you want to be that. You're not going to last with that; you're not going to be a fucking life coach. Whose life could you possibly help with? "That's exactly what she told me. I remember her words when she said that I wasn't going to be shit, and that I was never going to be as good as the new guy she'd found. I'd taken everything she had said on a personal. This was, because when I was with her, I was a good guy to her. I've helped her in a lot of ways, and that's the thanks I got back from her. As for my perspective on her afterwards, I don't think I can help her because she's a narcissist, and that's what narcissists do. But what I decided to do was to use my experience with her to teach others, and by doing so it actually helped me heal. In all that hurt, anger, and disappointment that I felt, I would channel that to produce some of the best content on what it's like to deal with someone who has narcissistic personality disorder, and I'd be one of the best to do that.

When I made my videos of my experience with her, I made it a point never to seriously bash her and never to

feed the emotions about how bad I was doing after I left her. I never made it a personal thing. I just stuck with the information. I didn't want to give her the satisfaction that I was going through all this because of her or because I was so beaten down from being in that situation. I didn't want to give her that thrill, that emotional victory that she would have enjoyed. I didn't want her to be like, "Hey, he still can't get over me, he can't forget me. He's making videos that talk about me. He's got to be missing or hurt for me. I bet he still wants me.
Yes, that's exactly how a narcissist thinks about it. They feel like you can't do without them. Even though I left her, in a narcissist's mind, you're going to pay for that. You will realize eventually how much of a mistake you made by leaving them, and they expect you to come back. They expect you to fail at whatever you do. They expect you to still have a longing for them, to hurt for them, and to miss them. But there is no way! I was going to cry about spilled milk and go out like that. I wasn't going to become an emotional wreck because I was manipulated, lied to, cheated on, disrespected, and a variety of other things that's too long to list. I just made up my mind that I'm going to be successful from my experience with her, and that I'm never going to look back again.

I am not going to be here talking like I was just this tough guy and it was an easy thing to overcome. Where there times that I wanted to reach out to call her? Yes! Absolutely! Did I feel that there was no closure and I had to say something to get that closure? Yes, I did! But the thing that I did not want to do was to go back to whining and crying about a decision that I made and needing to get away from her. That wouldn’t do me any good. In fact, it would open me up to being maliciously attacked by the narcissist. Because either a narcissist discards you or you leave them, especially if you leave them, to go back to them or to think that you will be with them again, is like walking yourself to the slaughter house. When you leave the narcissist and you're gone, you've got to stay gone.

I often say to people that one of the greatest things they can do when they have left a narcissist or discarded is to try to put themselves in a position to do things or to make certain achievements on the basis of their own efforts. Why is that important? It's because it's building up self-esteem that's been torn down by the narcissist. It rebuilds the trust that was crushed by the narcissist. Whenever you leave one of these toxic narcissistic situations, you will have to work on and repair the damage done. And one of the best ways to do that is to begin to achieve and do things in a productive and progressive manner afterwards.

As for me, she lit a fire in me, by making a mockery and a fool out of me. What she did had made me go to a zone or a mode I've never seen from myself. I was surprised. My focus was on sharp razor. All I could think of was how do I make the right changes in myself to get back on track from where I had fallen off. Now I've had clients coming in consistently, and I've had an e-course audio that's selling pretty well. I was now looking for something else to work on, which would further put me on the road to achieving the ultimate success that I had set out to complete for myself.

Interpretation

When you get to a point of realization from what you've gone through in any toxic situation, especially if you've dealt with a narcissist, the only thing you can do is take responsibility for your part, your role, and get yourself back in alignment and remove yourself from being involved. That's if it's at least in a traditional relationship. If not, you may not have had any choice, especially if you have parents or caregivers who were narcissists. Again, one thing you can do is make yourself the absolute best person you can be. Don't be afraid of failure; don't be afraid of what others will say about you. Don't let anything sabotage you while trying to do to make yourself a better person. Do you realize that today, in this word, your mere existence makes you a winner? Do you realize that you had to win against millions other sperm to be the first to fertilize your mother's egg to be in this world today? You're already a winner; you've come to the world to be a winner. Now you just have to start acting as a winner, and when you realize that, you will start to see victories.

Every part of success involves a positive way of thinking and a mindset that will carry you forward; it determines whether or not you will succeed, or whether or not you will fail. One thing is for sure, a broken mind will get you nowhere, and it won't make you see anything good in your life. In fact, you're going to see the same things happen over and over in your life. Negative attitudes and bad habits must be replaced with positive attitudes and good habits. Attitudes are, critical in determining the outcomes of the paths you take My point is, take a stand to overcome adversity with unwavering faith and being relentless in your pursuit in whatever you are trying to achieve even if you have to utilize something or someone to motivate you, channel that energy into something that will produce the best result for you.

Chapter 10: Here Comes the Opportunities

I was really starting to get adjusted to my new apartment. My mind was in a much better place now that I no longer had to deal with the stress of living in my car. My YouTube channel was starting to grow more popularly, and I was starting to see a lot more money flowing in. My belief in YouTube was starting to pay off, and it was pushing me to see other ideas that I wanted to see come to fruition. Eight months later, I came up with the idea that I had for a documentary dealing with narcissists. The premise of the documentary would be to apply all the information I had gathered from being with my ex. I would include the re-enactment on film using actors while I was narrating.

It was an excellent idea for me to give a visual picture of what dealing with a narcissist would look like a form and an outside perspective. Those who had dealt with a narcissist would relate, because I would show how circumstances and events play themselves out on film. The only problem I had was that at the time, I didn't have enough finances to pull the idea off. So, I made a video on my YouTube channel, discussing the idea that I was thinking about producing a documentary and my intention to start a go-fund-me account to get the capital to pay for the documentary. I had a good response from the audience initially and everything went well for about a month. I collected about six hundred and twenty-three dollars, which was not enough for all that I wanted to do for the documentary. In the meantime, until I got enough money to fund the documentary, I'd just have to keep pushing to fund the plan and make money from my YouTube channel, consulting services and my audio e-course, all of which went well. Between the three, I might be able to get enough money to put the documentary together. For now, those plans will have to be put on the back burner, as I started putting more time into my consultations, which also helped me to add more consistent content to my YouTube channel.

Over a short period of time, during these consultations, I heard some of the most outrageous situations from individuals professing to have been with narcissists and what they had gone through. Believe it or not, giving people advice as a life coach and narcissistic survivor has also become my own therapy. I can't tell you how many times I was getting confirmation or deeper insight from listening to some of my client stories. For the first time, I've heard the things that I've been through with my ex narcissistic girlfriend from the mouths of other people who have been dealing with similar situations. These were people from all walks of life and profession who had encounters with these narcissistic people or people who at least believed they were with narcissists.

One thing I've always done to make sure I'm on track and not going far beyond the scale of understanding narcissism has always been to read, crosscheck and re-

evaluate the things I've come up with from my experience with the narcissist by discussing my theories with doctors who have been in the field of psychology. I would compare the knowledge of my experience with the knowledge that these doctors had from an academic point of view. Most of the time, all that I've learned was adding up to be accurate in a real way.
Cognitive dissonance, which is often very common when dealing with toxic situations, especially with a narcissistic individual, has begun to disappear. I started to see the pattern of how narcissists were moving, and the alignment was spot on with how my ex was. So, I knew I was on the right track. Also, I knew how to articulate and get the message out so that people understood it, making it highly relatable and effective for people to gain understanding.

One day, while I was reflecting and thinking about my life, how far I've come since I left, which wasn't a lot of time, I realized that I was doing better than what I was doing while I was with the narcissist. Eventually, I decide to reach out to the lady that Dr. Griffin told me about. I reached out to her, and she responded.
I said “Hey, this is Quinn! Dr Griffin had been telling me about you. He said I should give you a call”.

“Oh… hey, Quinn! Man, I have been following your work and you have helped me through a lot of things that I am going through from my ex narcissist’, she said

“Thank you” I replied, showing my gratitude.

“I was reaching out and wanted to know if you would be in a short film that I was producing about my situation with the narcissist that I was with. I need somebody to play my therapist in the film. We are filming tomorrow; can you make it?” she asked.

“Sure, I would love to have that opportunity. This sounds good to me.” I responded.

“Fine, the only catch is you would have to memorize the script by tomorrow because I want to shoot the scene while I have access to the camera crew I am working with”, she said.

“Wow… okay, if the script isn’t too bad, I am sure I can catch on to it. I will try my best but I definitely don’t want to miss out on this opportunity. So yes, send me the script” I responded.

She told me “Don’t worry about it, it won’t be too much. We can go over some things and kind of improvise as needed.”
“That sounds good. I will be waiting on the script”, I said.

“I will send it to you as soon as I get back home. I will send you a copy and we will go over it later”, she said

I ended the call, and when the call was over; my thought to myself was that I didn't expect this. I've been stopping myself from talking to this lady all this time Dr. Griffin told me she wanted to talk to me. But I was so busy trying to catch up on everything I had on my YouTube channel that I didn't even bother about it. Now that I've reached out, I've just been in shock and amazement at how ironic it is. I'm trying to make a documentary, and then I'm running into a woman who's making a film. It's like things were coming together to guide me into what I was actually trying to get involved with, which was the documentary I was trying to put out. I was so thrilled that I forgot to get her name. I texted her saying, "Hey, I haven't picked up your name."

"It's Grace", she replied.

"Hey Grace, I know I introduced myself to you and you told me your name but I was so excited that I forgot. I wanted to make sure I remembered", I responded.

"It's not a problem", she texted back.

I have never acted a day in my life before and I did not know anything about being on set, but I was more than ready for the challenge of getting myself involved with Grace's project.

Later that night, she texted me, saying, "Hey! I'm going to send you the script. Can I get your email address, please? "I sent her my email, and soon enough, she sent the script. It wasn't too much, but it was enough for someone who had never been through a script or anything before. It's all been new to me. I had to learn to go; or, as people say, I had to learn on the fly. I called her when I received the script. She asked me if I had the script.
"Yes, I do have it. Do I have to memorize it in that way?" I asked.

"No, it's kind of improvising. You kind of go with the flow so that it comes natural", she answered.

"Okay, I think I can try that, after all I have been a life coach and I have been speaking about this. So, it shouldn't be too much of an adjustment for me to catch on and pull this therapy scene off", I said.

We spent about the next three or so hours practicing reading over the script, back and forth. I was already tired from doing stuff earlier that day. I decided to give it some rest, get up early in the morning, pick back the script and then head for the shoot which was around 3pm the next day.

I remember getting up early in the morning looking for a suit to wear, worried about how I was going to dress. I mean, Grace gave me a guideline as to what my wardrobe was supposed to be on the set, but I just wanted to make sure the look was natural. So, I picked up my gray sports coat and some jeans that I just threw on. I wanted to be relaxed and comfortable, but I also wanted to be professional.

I got dressed, and I headed over to the location where we were going to shoot the scene. I remember pulling up, nervous as hell. "Wow, what did I get into myself? I can't believe I 'm going to be acting in this short film, "I thought to myself. To be honest, I was a nervous wreck, but there was no turning back for me. This was an opportunity for me to do bigger things. I didn't know exactly what I was going to get out of it, but I was willing to wait and see ... I just had to do my part of it. Once I got on the set, I met all the camera crew, the actors and the actresses who were part of the project.

I got on my script and started reading it. The director told me where we were going to shoot, and how he wanted me to be on set, how I was going to fix my face to the camera. It's all been new to me. It was like learning as you go. It's something I've never done before. You know, I've been taking notes diligently because this is what I've been looking to do with my documentary idea. It was right up my alley to learn how to put things together. You know, I didn't know how I was going to do it, but I just knew I was going to make a documentary about my experience. I want to get a glimpse of being on a set is like and pay attention to how it's done.

This was priceless information for me, and I took it all in; from how the lightening was set up, how the scene was, to everything I could possibly learn. I remember the director saying "take your places" and I got my script trying to recall and make an effort to say all the lines I could remember. I remember the director said, "Do it as if you were with one of your clients." Well, I did it that way. Don't forget that I still had to stay on the script so I could have some continuity in the editing process. When it's time to edit, they've got to be able to pick up my words exactly so that they can know what's going on. So, when they said “action!” I just flowed off what I knew. Although I had memorized a lot, I only had one day to memorize most of these lines. So, it was kind of jumpy at times. I remember there were a lot of cuts and stops because I was forgetting some of my lines. Nevertheless, we got it and it took us about two hours to finish. It was my first acting role as a therapist. It was quite interesting and fun.

Once we were done, I was talking to one of the camera guys, I said, "Man, this is a nice piece of equipment you've got." We started talking about lighting for the video shoot, how it was going to be set up and other things. He asked me what else I do for work besides filming.

"I am a life coach. I met Grace through Dr Griffin. He referred me to her" I answered".

"Okay, that's interesting", he remarked.
"Yeah, in fact I actually want to shoot my own documentary", I said.

"If you are trying to shoot, I am the guy for you. I got the lighting and everything; I have another guy here that does the sound. We can do your documentary for you", He replied.

"Really?" I asked

"We do some of the best work out of here. Take my number", he said pitching his work to me.

I took his number and said "That's excellent. I am definitely hitting you up and getting back to you. Then we can talk pricing and other things like that"

"Absolutely, give me a call" he responded.

Afterwards, I thanked Grace for allowing me to be part of her project. I remember going back home with the biggest grin on my face, saying to myself, "I just finished my first acting role and it was fun. I've had a lot of fun doing that. Wow! Wow! Wow! All these things are going to happen to me back to the back. I got the blessings coming in unexpectedly. I met someone in the film industry who was a videographer. I didn't have to go out myself to get it, but it came to me instead. I didn't have to go and look for it.

It's been about a month, and I reached out to the film guy. I told him, "Hey man, I'm Quinn. I'm the guy who played the therapist in Grace's short film.

"Yes, I remember you," he said.

"Hey, look man, I want to shoot a documentary, but I don't want to break the bank, but I want to shoot something of great quality about my experience with a narcissist."

“We don’t charge much. I charge by the hour but it shouldn’t be too much. We will work out something” he said.

“Better, yet let’s meet up and sit down in person and talk about it”, I requested.

“Fine we can do that”, he said accepting the offer to meet with me in person.

I set up a date and a time, and I remember going to the area I used to visit while I was looking for interviews. They always had office spaces, and some of them were open. I was asking about it. I was trying to make my interview and meetings with people more formal. They said they've had an opening at one of the office locations, but it's been running for so much a month, and they've got a special — you signed up for a year, and you get two months off. I couldn't beat that offer to get a place to hold my personal meetings and consultations with people. I went on ahead and I signed up. I remember it was on the first floor, and they had a place where you could have your company listing in the directory of the building. That was just perfect for me. I had a good spot in the building, on the first floor with a spectaculars view. It was been excellent!

I went on to get my company officially licensed and incorporated. So, I was now formally incorporated as ASSC Direct. I remember the time I took the keys to my office and I was smiling. It's been so real. I was now fully incorporated with my own office in a suite with other offices inside of it. My vision into what I wanted to do moving forward was coming at God's speed. Everything was flowing well. I met the film guy at the office about a week later, we talked over everything I wanted to do with the documentary, we came up with a reasonable price and I locked him in with the crew that I needed with a down payment to make sure he would be available when I needed him. I gave him the date, time range that I wanted to shoot and film this. Then I began to work on putting together the documentary together. I had to come up with a plan for my idea of what I wanted to do. I hired a receptionist to help me with my bookings, appointments and putting things in order. That's not a strong point of mine when I had so many other things I was doing right now, my life had turned into a busy one, but it was a busy one, and I enjoyed it because I was productive.

Now, as soon as I started to get all the things I needed in place, the farthest thing on my mind was my ex-narcissist, and I'm going to tell you why. Because I was busy; I was busy being productive, I didn't have time to really think about her or what I was going through with her. Although I was hurt with the things she did to me, yet I was transforming in such a way that I was becoming more than I was when I was with her that she was becoming a distant memory. You might have heard many times that success is the ultimate revenge. For many of you who have not experienced this in the way of becoming successful, I can attest it truly is the ultimate revenge. And let's not even focus on the revenge part, but just the feeling of being fulfilled within yourself starts to take over once you start to accomplish things. Now, she was fading and fading so much out of my memory. I've met many different people, and I've had conversations with numerous different people. My life, as it was when I was with her, was no longer the same; so, my feelings had changed and were no longer the same for her.

For me, this was the beginning of something special that I've been embarking on. And it could only get better in my mind as to how it all went. It was almost like it was meant to be like that. It was like I was meant to do this.

Interpretation

There is a lot of power in achievement. People may not know it, but as you begin to achieve and accomplish things it becomes easier to deal with whatever you might have gone through that may have been unpleasant to you or might have been traumatic. Once you begin to get productive and put in your time and energy into a lot of things and getting better or accomplishing something, it takes a lot of that pain and agony away. Many times, when we think about our exes that are narcissists, we reminiscence frequently because we don't have anything else to fill that void. We don't have life outside of what we were making while we were with them. That is a limiting mindset, because it still keeps you enslaved to the individual who is no longer around but still has such a strong hold on your mind and emotions. You can't fully move on because you are still dragging and longing for them.

My remedy was to invest myself into building, learning and educating myself. As I was doing more tings to put myself in a better position, it was adding value to me. As I added value to myself, I started to understand the value of me and what I was capable of. So, the entire negative thing that my ex-girlfriend was telling me about what I would not become and what I wouldn't achieve was being discredited by my actions to better my own self.

Remember this, your efforts your work, your determination will be what determine your worth. But I have to say this; don't do things to prove a point to them. When I say them, I mean the exes that you may have left or gotten rid of. Do it to prove a point to yourself; do it to prove that you are capable. You are worth it. Once you begin to develop that mind set, you will start experiencing those things that comes with that mindset. If you have a winner's mindset, you will start experiencing things that comes with a winner's mindset. If you have a loser mindset, you will start experiencing things that comes with a loser's mindset. Attitude is everything; and when you start to put out being productive and being busy with things that give you joy and happiness, you will realize that all of those things comes from within and that you are truly the author of your destiny.

Chapter 11: Realizing My Purpose

After meeting the film guy-Sylvester and ironing out all the details of how I was going to make this documentary, I came to realize that I'd need a lot more stuff to put in place to pull the documentary off. These things were mainly locations, actors and actresses. I had to make all these things come together. What we did was to formulate a plan about how I was going to materialize the idea I had for this documentary. That meant I had to pause a little more until I got the budget to secure location, actors, and other things like that. This pushed the project back to about six months from the initial meeting we had with regard to filming and producing this documentary project. This is my first time ever to put something like his together. I didn't have any experience; I just had a vision of what I was going to do and how I was going to see it coming out.

I've now reached out to Grace again since she's been involved in filming and producing. I needed some information from her about how I could bring things together for my documentary. These things were like references to actors that she might have used in her project that I could use. Grace was a very resourceful and knowledgeable person with a lot of connections, and that worked well for me because she was able to find the location and the people that were needed to help put the documentary together in a way that I was at least looking to make happen. When I spoke to Grace I said, "Hey

Grace, I 'm looking at producing my own project, which is going to be more of a documentary, where I have actors acting out certain scenes to go along with the documentary, while I'm narrating parts of what I'm illustrating."

“Oh… okay! When are you looking to do this?” She asked.

“I don’t have an exact date or time put in place now, but with the way it’s looking right now, probably about six months from now”, I replied.

She asked again “Where do you need me to help you out? What type of help are you looking for?”

"I was thinking maybe I could get some of the actors that you used to get into my project. I don't have a lot of budget, but while we're on set, I'm going to make sure we all eat. I'm going to make sure that everything is taken care of if they show up and we're going to go from there, "I said, laying bare my mind.
She said “cool, I would love to be a part of it. I can even be in it myself. I don’t mind doing that myself.”

“Okay cool then”, I responded.

“Do you have a script, the acting and stuff?” she asked.

ıaven't got that yet. I 'm working on it and I can ɔly have it in a month or two as I figure out exactly ⁄ I want to put the documentary together, "I replied.
Okay fine, that sounds good to me. Let me reach out to a couple of people and let them get in touch with you and then you can go from there" she said.

"That sounds pretty good. I 'm looking forward to it. If there's anything else you might need from me, let me know. Thank you, Grace; thank you for your help and time, "I said, expressing my appreciation to her.

Outside of Grace, I was still looking for actors and actresses on my own. I reached out to a couple of agencies that were just starting out and were trying to get their foot out with their actors and actresses. So, I found an agency where the lady's name was Randa. I reached out to her and I told her what I was doing with my project and what I intended to get done. She said "I may have one or two actresses that you can look at.

"Why don't you go to the website to see the portfolios that the agency has for actors and actresses? You might find something that fits the need you're looking for, "she said.
"Cool, I'm going to take a look at that. I'm going to look at it. I'll get in touch with you when I'm ready to make an interview and let you know the kind of actors and actresses I 'm looking for, "I said.

"That sounds good," she said, concluding the conversation.
After going through the website, I found about three that I was interested in, but I stuck with two that I thought I could actually use in the documentary. After making my choice, I sent her an email saying, "Hey, I like the two of them."

"I will let them know if you can send them the script", she replied.

At the time, I didn't have a full script, but I put something together that was on the line of what I wanted to see, and I sent it to her.
"Give me the date and time you want them to be there, and I'll make sure they're there in time for the audition," she said. We then set it up and confirmed the dates and times.

Looking back on it, I didn't have a clue as to what I was doing about making a film. I just had an idea and a vision of what I wanted to see, as I said before. To make up for my lack of knowledge, I started reading books about how to produce and direct, how to put together a film casting, how to structure a film production. This means working together with those who would be on the scene to make sure things go smoothly. This also means that I had to be in close communication with my videographer to let him know what I was thinking, so that he could have the right equipment and the right lighting for these particular scenes that I was trying to put together. By no means was it easy at all.

This added a lot more work to load the work to what I've already done with clients on my YouTube channel who wanted to consult on their situation with narcissists, and on top of that still remain consistent to make YouTube videos available. I've had a lot going on here. It was heavy on me, but I've still been driven by that purpose. I still had that burning desire in me to bring to fruition the things I had envisioned in my mind.

I started writing the script and scene blocking the way I wanted to see this documentary coming together. The premise of all this was based on what I had gone through and what I had experienced in my situation with the narcissist I had been with. So, the scenes were taken from my personal experience. Why was that so important to me? Well, I wanted to show people what it looks like to watch the narcissist's dysfunction being played out on film, while narrating to them what's going on in each scene to help them better understand what they were seeing. It was the perfect idea for this, and I truly believed that it would be well received by the audience.

About a week later, Grace came in contact with me and said she had a few people she wanted on board who were definitely interested. She asked if I could get a script for them. I said, "Yes, I can give them a script."

"I will give them your number, and they'll get in touch with you, and you guys can work out the details from there," she said.

"Thanks a lot Grace for your time, I owe you big time" I replied showing my unfettered appreciation for her help so far.

The thought on my mind was, "So it's still coming together." I really couldn't explain it at the time, but I just felt it was amazing. I had a vision of something that I wanted to do, based on an experience that was devastating to me, but now being worked out in such a way that I could share it and get it out to the masses, especially to my YouTube supporters who were going through the same thing that I was going through, and they wanted more answers, more clarity and understanding, and that was perfect.

I was now in a position where I wrote, produced and directed my very first film production. I remember the first time I met the actors and actresses and sat down in a meeting and got ready for auditions, I looked at everything, and the thought in my head was, "Wow, I can't believe I'm doing this. I'm in the director's seat; I'm about to put together a cast. "This was a mind blowing to me, because there I was a regular guy who was homeless at one point in time; now I'm in the director's seat about to put together a film production casting. Everyone who came to me was spectacular. It was like they were the perfect fit for what I was putting together for this documentary. The actors and actresses were full of energy, optimistic and vibrant. It didn't take long to complete the whole process, because the connection between all of us was just so wonderful and serendipitous. I managed to not have to spend so much on the actors. All I had to do was supply the food and the place and I would make sure there was something to eat all the time. We always had a good time together on the set. The majority of the budget went to the location and paid the film crew to put it together. So, if you want to talk about a blessing, getting six cast members to be part of this project and not having to pay for it was a phenomenal blessing.

Although there was one member of the documentary project who was an attorney- Mr. Ebler, whom I had to pay. His time was roughly about two hundred dollars for the hour during the interview. I got a wealth of knowledge from him for that hour and we became friends from that point on. He was very monumental to the progress of the project which I did not mind paying for him to be on. It was worth it. I was also blessed with the opportunity of having Dr. Griffin on the project too. We couldn't necessarily get him to the location to do the actual filming but he did provide a voice over for one of the scenes in the documentary. This was one of the important things that I needed to make this documentary come out the way I wanted it to be.

After all the interviews and auditions were done, I gave the cast about three weeks to prepare for the actual filming. You know, six months have passed since I met Sylvester-my lead videographer. I told him I needed six months to put a few things in place. So now I had to secure the location where we were going to film the scenes for the documentary. Grace came back with her resourcefulness with a man who had a food truck and was willing to let us use his food truck to shoot one of the scenes at the park at night. That was another wonderful benefit of having someone like Grace on the team, helping out with what she could do; and she did it all for free. Grace has a very good heart, and I will always be thankful for all that she has done for me.

The directing part came naturally to me once we started filming. Putting everything in place and thinking about how the project was coming together and other things that had to be done didn't seem as hard as I was afraid of once we started filming. I had a lot of help from my videographer, Sylvester. I learned how everything was supposed to work, including lighting and other things relatable to filming. That was a good thing because I didn't have a clue of how a lot of this stuff went, but I was learning as I went through the process. This filming thing was another part of my therapy. I loved being on the set; I loved being productive and doing something positive. Creating something that I put together, which started out as a thought, an idea and became a reality, feels very powerful, especially in the process of recovering from something that was hurtful in your past. On average, we were on set for about four hours, and this was for filming just one scene of five to ten-minutes. It's a lot of work that goes into filming and producing, making sure everything is all right and having to go over and correct things. It's a lot of work, but it still was teaching me valuable things in my expansion of, not just being a life coach, but also a filmmaker.

Once all the scenes were filmed and done, the final part was the editing. Editing was another thing that I didn't know how to do, but I was able to sit in with my videographer going through every scene, cutting and editing every particular scene the way I had envisioned it. After we finished the post production, I got the copyright. Then came the time to start marketing and put it out there. I was trying to make sure I had a good quality product that I could present to people that they would not only enjoy, but most importantly learn from. I made some submissions to film festivals as well once we were done with the project.

There's a precarious story about my documentary submission to the film festivals, which I submitted to a

California-based Hollywood company. They were looking for a short film of about fifteen minutes. My documentary was about an hour in time length... I didn't read between the lines at the time I submitted my documentary, which should have been disqualified my submission because it was a 15-minutes over the benchmark, but they accepted it anyway. I 'm going to get to this point later, but I want to digress briefly to the point where I have to market the documentary and release it to my YouTube audience.

I had to pay for YouTube ads so that the documentary would pop up in a commercial format. I had to tell my audience that I had a documentary coming out, but it wasn't released yet. I showed them a short preview and it was very well received. People were looking into it when the documentary was released. A lot of people started buying it. They loved the documentary and said it was very informative. There were a lot of high praises coming in that made me feel good about what I had produced.

As I said before when I was talking about the submission of my film to the film festival; I received an email saying that my documentary had been chosen from about 2,000 submissions and we won third place for Best Independent Documentary in 2018. At that point, I was overjoyed. I couldn't believe that. Wow! Wow! Wow! I didn't expect it to be that high in selection. By the way, I was up against people who had made films and had been in the film industry for years. Some of them had gone to school to study about filming. On top of that, I had submitted the wrong video time length timing which shouldn't have been accepted. But I felt that they must have watched it and drawn a conclusion that it was good enough regardless. Although it was in the wrong category, they still chose to give me the award anyways. Despite the fact that I had never produced a documentary before, the first time I did, I won an award. That was big time for me. It showed that not only was I doing well on YouTube by being informative, now I have found a new talent of being able to produce a documentary in film format that was just as worthy of high praise to the point of being award winning. You know, this comes from people who didn't know anything about me being a life coach or about me on my YouTube channel. For the first time, these were people who saw me and judged my quality film production along with the information. This was saying that I was in the top category with this information about narcissistic personality disorder. It officially came to me as being one of the best life coaches out there to do it. I told the team about what had happened: "Hey, we won an award. This year's 'Departure of Empathy' was the third place for independent documentary, 2018. They were all ecstatic. We've all gone wild with excitement. None of us saw it coming, so it was huge to us.

It was the first time you got an award. It was time for me to move on to the next thing, and I would do that by putting together a tour where I would choose different cities to go to where I would talk to the followers of my YouTube channel. I was trying to connect with the people more. I wanted to be able to see those people, who were going through the stages of recovery from narcissistic abuse, and I wanted to be able to connect with them in person, and now I wanted to give them the information in person. It's one thing to talk to people in videos and put it on YouTube; it's another thing to be able to shake hands and hug people in person who admire your work and value what you do. That's what motivated me to put the tour together. I remember the first time I mentioned it on my YouTube channel telling people that I was thinking about putting together a tour and asking for their opinion. I got a lot of people who responded with excitement, saying, "Yes, we'd love it. Let us know when it's going to happen.

It was a great joy for me to know that people actually wanted to see me come out and interact with them and tell them my story and give them advice. It made me feel good about it. At this point, I had a full-fledged film crew hitting it off well with my videographer Sylvester. We've also become close friends. I put him in on the idea of going on a tour, and he's coming along at one or two locations I've been talking to record this event. He was more than willing and excited about the opportunity. Once it was official, I put together an ad campaign and got in touch with my graphic artist who designed the ad for my new tour called "Quiet Weapons for Silent Wars against Narcissists' Tour." I started putting together the necessary information about the tour and what it was going to be like. I got back with Sylvester again and did a short video of what I was going to be speaking about with me about the on this tour, so that people knew what they were going to get out of it. It went pretty well. Tickets were made accessible to people who wanted to attend and sold out pretty quickly. It was like in a new type of success found that was coming in so fast and moving quickly towards me that I had to sit down to take a break.

One day while I was in my office I got a call that came in. I answered and what do you know, it was my ex narcissist girlfriend. The call was totally unexpected and all I said, was what do you want?

“I have a lot of animosity towards you Quinn. I didn’t think you cared about me at the time”, she said.

“Well, I did care. I’ve moved on now, what do you want from me?” I responded. She told me she had a family and had a kid with this guy and told me about all that she was going through. I told her good luck with that and before I hung up, she said “I still love you and it sucks.” I ended the call.

"You have to be kidding me, I thought to myself. You called to tell me you're still in love with me, and it sucks? After all the shit you've been talking about me? "You know, she still had some of those ugly words while we were still talking too because I didn't reciprocate any desire for her back.
She said during the conversation, "What are you now? Are you supposed to be a life coach? Helping people, huh? I can't see how you're going to help people. Please tell me how you can help people, because I can't see it.

I answered her by asking, "Well, you're obviously following my YouTube channel." She said yes. "You see the subscribers I have, don't you? "She replied," Yes "again. Then I said they were already talking about my success. "Go to the comment section and read for yourself, and I'm pretty sure you can figure out how I'm helping people out."

She didn't say anything. I left the conversation by saying "Hey, I am glad you found a family, but I don't have anything for you. I have moved on; in fact, I don't have a lot of time to think about you. I have moved past that. I have to go now" and I ended the call.

That call said a lot to me. I was so far removed from the mental space that I was in while I was, with her that it brought me back to the memory of thinking that at one point, I had made a mistake by being with her and to now realize that I had actually won. Not that it was a race or that I was competing to prove a point to her, but I actually made the right decision more than anything by leaving her ass alone. It was a blessing to leave her; staying with her, I was destined to be destroyed by her. Well, you know what? It brought a little more closure in this strange way. When you're happy, and if you've really content, and you've moved on with your life, there's no reason to get back to the past with an ex, especially because you've once been with that you didn't feel like was good for you. It was foretelling to me that she wasn't doing well, and that she probably got into a situation that she regrets and wants me to have sympathy for her. You know, she's watching me on my YouTube channel all the time. She's seeing the progress and success that I've had going on in my life with her not being included, and I've never looked back. I never wanted to be back with her at that point in time, and for the first time I was feeling free and clear from the narcissist. She reached out to me and it brought a lot about healing and closure. Now I've started to embrace my goal of healing other people and helping others to get that close and understanding, so that they can move on and have a better life.

I started to feel that there was a reason why I had to meet her, why I had to go through all the things that I went through with her to receive the blessings that I was receiving from being with her. I've never stooped down to her level; even on my YouTube videos, I've never done anything to degrade her. I'm just putting out the information. By moving forward and accepting the situation I was faced with, I found my goal; my goal of helping and healing others. What a wonderful thing to be used to improve other people, to help them find their way, to help them move forward in life, and hopefully to discover their purpose as well.

Interpretation

Sometimes, when we go through things, we're going to get involved and do what we have to do. Maybe we really don't know the meaning or why we're necessarily going through it, but we're just going along with it. Sometimes, God has a message and a plan in the midst of all these adversities, and that message, if you listen well enough to it, can lead you right to the purpose you're meant to be working out of. I was not going back to seek revenge or anything like that from the ex-narcissist, because I was the bigger person outside the situation I had with her, I was rewarded. I have to say that rewards don't come without effort though, and you have to be willing to make an effort and push to prepare yourself for the reward. A negative mind doesn't have the same vision as a positive mind to see where it's going and how to get there. When you operate in a positive way of thinking and have a positive vision, it produces positive things. Through my diligence and not allowing those things to overwhelm me, I was able to get the closure that I needed. Now, you might say, "They're never sorry," but they don't have to be really. When you truly heal and live in your purpose, it negates the need for an apology. Always find a way to realize that and to live in your purpose. Find what gives you joy; find what brings you peace of mind and find what satisfies you to the end of your being. You know what this is doing? It produces that happiness that allows you to recognize that peace and love within you.

Chapter 12: Discovering What Changed Me

With three years of my life withdrew from the ex-narcissist, and while I was on my way to healing, I began to have a deep understanding of why some people came into your life and why they were put there. I realized that there are people out there for reasons, seasons, and a lifetime. I believe that my ex-narcissist has definitely been put into my life for a reason, and that reason has become apparent. In the process of trying to destroy me mentally and emotionally, I found a way to turn my pain into fulfillment, and my sadness into happiness. Throughout this whole ordeal, I've had time to reflect and access my life in general. I realized that I wasn't raised in the healthiest environment as a child growing up. On top of that, my grandma, who was very helpful in raising me, was a sociopath. There were times when I was growing up around her, when I was wondering if she even liked me as her grandchild. She wasn't really expressive, so love was something she'd hardly ever show me unless I did a favor for her or something that would directly benefit her, or maybe I would get a pat on the back.

Growing up in that environment, my grandma conditioned me to be an appropriate source for narcissistic women in general. Not only was I conditioned to love this type of woman, but I also normalized the behaviors and tactics that were used to emotionally confuse me as a child. I was never really aware of these things until I was confronted with a situation that called for me to do a lot of research and reflection. Sometimes, to get to that point of fixing yourself, you have to be so far removed from what you used to be as a person to be able to identify the key underlying issues in your life that first produced it. I started to see things that didn't work out well for me while I was growing up and why I was going through life with so many insecurities and failures stemming from dysfunctional family support that I was receiving as a child.

Evaluating everything that I had been through with my ex-narcissist and moving towards a better quality of life, I was able to better understand the internal issues within myself that attracted me to women who would constantly disappoint me and show some of the toxic characteristics that I had become accustomed to seeing from my grandma. Once I was able to identify these behaviors, I started working on myself and changed the way I saw things in life in general. It was like I had to learn everything from scratch, and I had to learn healthy relationships and identify people who were genuine with good intentions. Everything was starting to make a lot more sense in terms of the women I've been attracted to and the kind of toxic behaviors in women that I put up with. It's all rooted in my childhood experience. Once I began to recognize and accept that, I was now able to begin to identify specific behaviors that I needed to work on, which made me an enabler for the narcissistic type of women. I was able to correct the things that made me choose and accept narcissistic women.

Coming to the realization that I was molded from a child to give all women the benefit of doubt, and them being defenseless and needy for protection from a man; I actually opened myself up to women who prey on the caring, loving nature and the hearts of good men who think and believe in this way about all women. On the contrary, the only woman who would not be prone to becoming toxic in this way would more than likely have been due to a significant increase in exposure to healthy family dynamics. But in general, this can be said for both males and females who have been properly raised.

I started to get a good understanding that my own boundaries were out of order. When I thought back to the whole time that I was involved with women, I began to see patterns in my behavior that helped to draw and promote toxic behaviors in those women that I chose to engage in or be in a relationship with. As I began to dig deeper to understand who I was as a person and the things I had been through, I came across some co-dependency information. Just to explain briefly, a co-dependent is a person who makes it possible for another person to be addicted, to have poor mental health, to be immature and irresponsible, etc. People who are prone to being co-dependent are people who have grown up quickly and are often forced into higher levels of responsibility. This can happen in situations where the parents of the child were not responsible, neglectful. In some cases, it could happen if the child, who might have been the only child or the first child, had to be the one who was looking out for the parents, or did some tasks, or had to watch out for the actions of the parents as a child, and the child had to be the first to react and prevent things that could affect them because of the neglect or unreasonable behavior of their parents. They may also not have received adequate support from their parents and caretakers.

As soon as the child grows up to be an adult, and is exposed to this type of family dynamics where the child has had to play the role of the responsible adult so to speak, the effects of a lopsided upbringing become apparent. It could have been because their parents or caretakers were not properly equipped for parenting; and that is not to say they were abusive, but they could have been immature parents, or they might have been careless, as I said before. The child will grow up with a certain anxiety about wanting to make sure everything goes right. This is bound to happen because, since childhood, they have been put in a position of having to be a caretaker or a fixer trying to make sure that everything is going well and that nothing is going wrong. So, as soon as the individual becomes an adult, they begin to attract people who need to be fixed, who need someone to rely on. This is where I found myself – to be a fixer, a caretaker from my childhood experience.

It always seemed like I was drawn to women who needed some kind of intervention, whose lives were totally dysfunctional. Yet, I would allow myself to come in and try to correct the situation, try to build them up, and try to help them overcome any shortcomings they had experienced. Time and time again, I was always getting the same result in the end. Trying to spend my time and energy trying to love and be right for someone who would ultimately take me for granted, not appreciate me, and in the end devalue me and discard me. It was the, the same result over and over again. And I just couldn't see that. I didn't understand that at the time though. I blamed myself for it; maybe I wasn't trying hard enough, or I wasn't doing well enough because of what they wanted to do that I wasn't willing to do.

This was, of course, me in the process of looking back in hindsight, which was a case of getting used over and over again. I didn't see the problem, however, because I was used to growing up that way. I have not seen the dysfunction; therefore, I have not been able to correct or correct it. I was blind to the fact that I had a problem that allowed this to happen again and again. But then I had a moment of light that popped up so strongly in my mind for me that the things I was reading about that gave me insight on co-dependency. This understanding would change my life forever, because as I began to gain this new knowledge, I started to change, and I started to set up a system based on new values that I didn't have before.

This new value system would cause me to operate in a different way that wouldn't lead me to the same patterns that would put me in a vulnerable position of being hurt or disappointed. So, the first thing I did was to create my own personal constitution and that was like a set of laws that I would abide by based on the set of principles that I valued, the things that I felt were important to me that I would give out but yet never receive in return. I made no exemptions to these rules and I made these rules above myself so that I had to answer to myself. If a person I was dealing with could not respect them, then there will be no more dealings with that person. I began writing down all the things that I liked and did not like. I started with things that were important to me and things that weren't important to me. These were all included and, of course, I have the expectations that have also been restructured. Now, all of these really talk about having boundaries in your life, and this is what I've been setting up for myself for the first time. They were new boundaries that included a completely different process of vetting people that I would allow my life to move forward. I no longer accepted and opened myself to people I just liked. No, that's over. Now, I was only allowing people who had a certain commonality in moral principles to be in my circle.

This was so powerful because it changed my behavior and the way I was operating. That's the number one thing I could say that was so powerful in this newly discovered awakening that I've had that my behavior has also changed. I haven't been as accessible as I used to be. I was no longer giving people the benefit of doubt without allowing them to prove themselves to me. This was all helping me to protect myself from the things that used to make me a victim of the circumstance from my upbringing. As I began to apply these new values, principles, and boundaries, I began to notice something; and that was the kind of people I was having in my circle. My circle became much smaller because I was no longer open to the general public, so to speak. I was now a private sector that was only able to allow an exclusive number of people who were worthy to be around me and to receive my time and attention. The unhealthy pattern has to be broken, and it starts with what you do to change yourself. If you want the same result, keep doing the same thing; but if you want a different result, you have to change what you do. That was what I had to do, and once I reformed myself from my old ways, I was able to see those changes.

Through all of these changes, I came to realize how much I was neglecting myself, how much I was putting others before me, and allowing myself to be mistreated or exploited in some cases. I see now, in a strange way, running into the ex-narcissist as a blessing because she was the catalyst for this change that I so badly needed in my life. I learned how to love myself by going through so much with her while I was in a transactional relationship with her. God works in mysterious ways, and I can attest that this is one of them. Turmoil, chaos and a lot of pain that I have gone through in my life have been a blessing at the end of a situation that has been a turning point for my rectification.

<u>Interpretation</u>

Why self-worth is often overlooked is beyond me. Sometimes, when we are put in a position where we have to look into the mirror and be real with ourselves, we would realize that we are the author of our situations, that we are in charge of our lives and that we are in control of the situations in which we find ourselves, and that we are the ones responsible for getting out of it. But it is also up to us to find a deeper meaning for ourselves, because that is where the meaning lies to make ourselves a better person. It starts from within. When self-reflection happens, change will undoubtedly happen as well. You can't be afraid to look at yourself and be honest and truthful about whom you are as a person. Pointing the finger is easy but doing the work so that you don't have to point a finger again is even harder. Many of us are too afraid to stand up to ourselves because we are afraid of what we will find within, but the only way to fix many of the problems that we face in life is to address it with ourselves.

So, I 'm telling you, don't be afraid to challenge yourself and go deep inside with your reflection. You'll be amazed at the answers you might receive to make a lifetime worth of change for you to move forward in life.

Chapter 13: Taking My Knowledge on The Road

With all the things I've learned about narcissism and the newfound things I've learned about myself, I felt it was time for me to go out and share this knowledge with the thousands of followers I have on my YouTube channel. I decided to set up a tour to be held in selected cities across the United States. This would give me the ability to speak to a live audience about my experience of dealing with a narcissist. I wanted to have more personal contact with my audience while presenting this information, and that would mean having an audience with whom to speak physically. It would also allow me to see some of the faces of those who have been victims of narcissistic abuse. I'll be able to meet and greet a lot of supporters who helped my channel grow, and this would give me a chance to thank them in person as well. This was the first time I had ever traveled to so many cities in my life in such a short time. So, putting everything together to make this happen was certainly a big deal for me, even though I had the help of my tour manager who helped put together the dates, times, and venues. It was still something that made me nervous because I had never done anything like that before.

Before I did this, I posed the question to my YouTube audience as to whether or not they would like me to make a live presentation. Surprisingly, in an overwhelming amount of responses, they felt it would be an excellent idea, and many said they would love to come and see it. From that point on, I knew that I had to make this happen. So, we started to get to the locations and times of each city. We had to determine the number of days I'd stay in each city. We put together an ad campaign to sell tickets for the events, which went very well. I believe we sold most of the tickets to the venues that we set up to deliver this lecture.

I remember how nervous I was at the very first lecture I gave. I've had anguish like crazy. Honestly, I've had butterflies in my stomach going on. I was wondering how the audience would receive me. I was nervous because it's one thing for you to make YouTube videos, and people are watching you, and it's another thing for them to be in front of you where you're talking and being asked questions. It's a whole different kind of thing I've never done that made me a little squeamish. Surprisingly, when I got up in front of everybody to talk, I just got into action and started to tell my story from the introduction to the background of how I got my knowledge, and so on. I could remember the intensity of the gazes on the faces of the audience staring at me; they took in every word I said. The interesting thing about this is that it made me feel comfortable. Afterwards, I didn't feel as nervous as I did, and I continued my presentation, which I kept as entertaining as possible.

The biggest thing I took away from this was the gratitude of fellow survivors of narcissistic personality disordered individuals. These people have been so grateful to me for sharing my story. A lot of them told me that they had healed and overcome the great adversity of what they had to go through with their ex-narcissists. For me, those were the moments that stuck and lasted the longest because I saw the faces and expressions of people I had never met in my life. From their stories, I could clearly understand the reasons for their lavish expression of gratitude. It made me feel good about helping people. I've been helping many overcome the harmful psychological afflictions of dealing with a narcissist who is a diabolical person that targets and hurts others, regardless of how the outcome is going to end or what condition they can leave someone in from their destructive ways. After my first lecture, I remember that my assistant came to me and said, "Those people seemed grateful to you and to the information you gave. It's changed a lot of their lives. They said they never knew that narcissists were affecting so many people. I said, "Most people don't even know what it is.

Most people don't even know they're dealing with narcissists, and they've been hurt so much by many of them. So, they're going out looking for answers to the questions, and they're going through someone like me with the information I'm giving out. That's what motivates me to continue to spread this knowledge to help others identify this disorder that goes unnoticed by the general society as a whole.

As we moved from town to town and met a number of people who were survivors of narcissistic abuse, I began to get a little overpowered from an emotional point of view, with the energy of people who were wounded and healed. It just made me realize how many people are hurting, but they're trying to get on with life while they're trying to get out of the way and get healed.

As I was sitting in my hotel room one night in one of the states where we were laid over in, I was just thinking to myself: "Man, people are really hurting out here, and when we look at the family dynamics where individuals come from. We've got to look at the root causes, and if we break that down, and not just look at it on the surface, we'd realize that a lot of this isn't from the individual we're encountering or dealing with that may have hurt us. We need to look at the connections from where these other individuals came from, because a lot of these people come from broken or dysfunctional households. So, if we point the accusatory fingers and say it's their fault, then we have to look at who was responsible for raising them. How have they been brought up? What also caused this dysfunctional individual to fail? Typically, when it's going on. You will have to look at who raised the parents, who raised this dysfunctional person, and it keeps going on and on. So, what we end up seeing is a cycle that has never broken, and a cycle is a continuum that leaves behind inseparable damage. It could come from neglect to spoil a child, abuse of a child, and many other things. The most important thing that has come to me is that it's about stopping the cycle. A lot of things we've learned haven't been properly taught by the caretakers that we've been responsible for. So, we're not going to point fingers. We need to learn how to address these issues.

A significant part of the narcissistic disorder comes from the environment. In fact, some scientists say there are some genetic components that contribute to this. But the type of environment that these people are raised brings an overwhelming amount. The more toxic the upbringing or the people they may be subject to being around, the more likely it is to produce some of the unhealthiest and least desirable traits in these individuals once they become full-grown adults.

I hear people sometimes say, when I'm describing how these disorders begin in the first place, they're going to say, "I grew up just fine"-talking about themselves. Well, what I'm always saying is that we all have a different threshold to what we can take. You may have a stronger tolerance for certain things that may not break down your psyche, that may not crush or cripple the functional part of your ego; while others may go through the same thing that you have gone through, and it completely crushes them. It's going to be based on each individual. We are not the same; therefore, we are not going to adapt and adjust to the conditions in exactly the same way that some others may do. Therefore, each individual will produce a different result or condition.

The narcissists are weak people; although they may appear strong and hard on the outside, they are very fragile. They're very delicate. Everything you can see and witness from those who seem to be confident and boastful is false. This isn't real. It's to protect them from the deeply embedded weaknesses they have inside, and this is part of understanding the disorder. The more you understand the disorder, the easier it is for you to heal someone who has a narcissistic personality disorder. This was the message I kept driving home and pushing forward on the tour. To get people to understand that healing is our responsibility at the end of the day, we need to push ourselves to overcome and heal so that we can move on properly from these traumatic experiences with narcissistic individuals.

As I was winding down my tour with about two cities left, fatigue began to set in. I've been doing a four-hour lecture in each city. It was starting to catch up with me when I was down to the last two cities. At that point, I wanted to go home. I see why the entertainers say how much they've missed their beds when they say how much they've been on the road for about six months; though,

I've been out for about two and a half months, and that seems like an eternity away from home. I was thankful that I had the opportunity to go out to do a tour of lectures on narcissistic personality disorder and to raise awareness among a lot of people. It's been very special to me.

Once the tour was over, I felt like I had made another major milestone in my life that I had never had a chance to do before. It was also in a strange way that I had the fear that I didn't know there was in me. One of them spoke in front of the people. Most people probably didn't notice that on the tour. The more people I spoke in front of, the better I got, the more confident I became. I also proved to myself that I was able to organize an event on a major level, at least for me, and to pull it off successfully. It seemed to me that I had arrived to be a narcissistic survivor expert coach. I was making a name for myself as one of the best people in the game to do it. I've always kept my approach straight to the point, not beating around the bush. I intentionally did that because I wanted people to feel like they were sitting across the table talking to their best friend. People really took to me by being that way. The information resonated with them, creating a healthy relationship that is still strong for me to this day. I am grateful to everyone who came out to listen to me, support me, and watch me share my story. It's something I'm never going to forget.

Interpretation

Overcoming the fear of failure has to do with taking the first step towards the very fear that you avoid in the first place. Initially, I didn't want to go on a tour, I didn't feel like it was needed, and that was mainly because of my fear that I was actually going out to meet people. I put it off and put it off until a close friend of mine pushed me to get me out of there. I took up the challenge, and I decided to go along with it.

There will be a time when you're going to have to push yourself to something that you might not want or that you might be afraid to do. You avoid it, and you avoid it until you begin to think it's impossible. Sometimes the very things you avoid hold the key to your advancement. Whether it's life, career, business, relationship, or whatever it may be, the things we fear are coming back to haunt us in the end, or we're going to have to face our fears at some point in this life we're living in. So why don't you take on that fear? Why not push yourself to the point where failure and fear are not a thing to have. This was something that I had to learn and I don’t regret it. I don’t regret pushing myself beyond what I could do because it paid major dividends for me and it helped me in my life in so many ways. It made me more friends. It made me more confident and made me more efficient in what I was already doing in the first place. Now I have a new found energy and approach to how I do these things. I am more motivated. I am less apprehensive. All of this at the end of the day has made me more successful. So, instead of doubting yourself, put yourself in positions to promote yourself.

Chapter 14: Putting It All Together

After returning home from the tour, I was finally able to get the much-needed rest. My body and my mind began to feel the effects of being constantly on the road. After two months of being away from home, I was so glad to see my bed again and sleep in it. I remember sitting in my room in amazement thinking about how I was able to do something that I had never dreamed of doing in my life. I traveled to multiple cities across the United States, met thousands of people, and was so far removed from the toxicity of what I had left when I was with the narcissist. I could not believe that I did all of these things in such a short period of time, yet I covered so much ground and moved into a totally new lifestyle. I've never dreamed of being a life coach specializing in narcissistic disorder, but I've been blessed up to this point and in my life sitting here being considered one of the best life coaches in the narcissistic recovery community. It made me realize for the first time that I was perhaps destined to do this. When I first started talking about my situation and what I was going through with my ex narcissist, making the first YouTube video, I had no idea that I would be a valuable source of information that people would look forward to hearing on a daily basis as I shared my experiences.

Throughout this, I have never taken into account how much I have had an impact on people's lives and how much I have had affected their recovery in dealing with narcissistic individuals and whatever the situation they have been in that hurt them. I was just trying to tell my story. I just wanted people to know that there are mindsets that are so diabolical, from individuals in the world who will prey on those whom they perceived to be weak, meek, friendly, or morally sound. They seek to take advantage of, or perhaps destroy, those who do not identify and detect the imposter within these individuals. The disorder of narcissistic personality is real. If you're going to meet a narcissist, that's something you'll never forget. It is something that leaves its residue in the psyche of the person who had to deal with it. I have heard people say many times, "Why haven't I caught this? Why me, huh? "They would have said that they weren't stupid, that they were intelligent. Still, they could not properly interpret what they were dealing with in their own situations.

The thing is, narcissists don't target your intellect, and no matter how intelligent you are, they won't stop you from being emotionally deceived or manipulated by a narcissist. They're playing on your emotions, and they're going to get through your emotions first. They know how to subtly entice your ego to the point of submission. The narcissist causes your own ego to fail you, because that's the first thing that lets them gain access to you. And it's also the first thing in the end that has a hard time letting the narcissist go when all is said and done.

At some point, anyone who has been a victim of narcissistic abuse will have to sit down with themselves and have that dreaded conversation with their ego and convince them by all means that the journey, the ride, the fun is over. It can be a very difficult thing to do, because your ego was having so much fun that it's hooked now, and you've become a junkie. Just like any other drug-specific habit, a person trying to kick that habit has to go through stages of recovery, and one of the most vexing stages is that withdrawal period when the body is eager for that thing that once gave it stimulating pleasure. It's no different from what the narcissist is. When you're done, some of you will still find yourself wanting to be with the narcissist. That was where I was initially, but through my journey, I had the opportunity to heal, not just myself, but others, while I was helping. One of the biggest things that kept me pushing all the way to recovery was that I knew I was helping others. On many accounts, I get emails from people telling me how much I saved their lives and how monumental I was in their recovery process. It was a testimony after a testimony, a message after a message I would read. You know what it did to me? It made me feel like I had to keep going with the information I was giving about the narcissistic personality disorder. I had to keep people aware of this disorder. Was my recovery process easy? No, it wasn't that. Even with all that I did with my business, travel, and my YouTube channel, there were still times when I had to go through regretting my experience with the narcissist.

I'll tell you one thing, there's nothing like the feeling of being healed from such a terrible experience. You'll know when you reach that point of recovery, because the overwhelming thoughts of what you've been through will begin to get duller and fade away. The intense emotions you feel will begin to subside as well. You're not going to be afraid to go to places you might have when you were with your ex-narcissist. It's just not going to matter anymore.

One thing for certain is that when you have experience of being with a person with a narcissistic personality disorder, things will be moving forward quite differently. At least, you'd have learned your lesson, because the way you look at friendships, partnerships, relationships will be different. The way you approach them will also change. Your mind will now shift to scrutinizing almost every person you've had to deal with or encounter. For me, I came to realize that I still trust my judgment and do not allow my interaction with the narcissists that I have had an impact on how I move forward in life. This kind of thinking really breaks down your own worth, your self-esteem, and your ability to trust your own judgment.

I looked at it this way: you can be one of two things when you come from experience-you can be a survivor or you can be a victim. I 'm pretty sure I didn't choose to be a victim; I chose to be a survivor. I chose to turn the experience I've had into a movement. I didn't want to be the man who was sitting back, crying and feeling bad, asking why the women were so bad. I knew better than that, and I knew the difference between a normal woman and a woman who has some kind of disorder. I think you should be constantly aware that you do not fall into the habit of generalizing and thinking that everyone you encounter is a narcissist. That would turn out to be a very unhealthful attitude to take forward in recovery. Life is one big classroom, and I've never known a student who's got every answer right. So, these experiences we're going through are for us to learn from and correct so that you don't make the same mistake over and over again. There have been many times in my healing process that I wanted revenge for being duped and used by the narcissist. But at some points I looked around at all the things I'd accomplished, and all the things I'd done in my life, all the places I'd traveled to, all the people I 'd met, that feeling went away. I was starting to realize that through my success, I was getting revenge. Part of that came one day with the confirmation of the ex-narcissist. She sent me an email asking me for a consultation. How ironic, I was thinking. This individual emails me asking for help and advice on what a narcissist can do to help themselves. Keep in mind that the ex-narcissist still had to watch my videos on YouTube; seeing every transition I had to go through to see that they didn't break me and couldn't crush me but wanted another chance to get back to me again. We call this "Reidolization" in the narcissistic community, because even when they did all those things to tear you down, which my ex-narcissist did, she didn't succeed. At the end of the day, because I wasn't stooping to the level of lowness that she had, I was able to rise above and be victorious.

Honestly, I was irritated when she reached out. I felt that this individual had the audacity to think that I would give her free advice without paying for all the things she had done to me? Did she really think everything's going to be all right and be glad to take her request for a consultation? No, absolutely not! I ignored her, and I never looked back. That was another major moment for me, the spelt of C-L-O-S-U-R-E. After all these years, the narcissists had never left. She was watching, hiding herself so I couldn't see her. Being the narcissistic expert that I am, I know that it was not really a matter of consulting her. It was more of a heat check because she saw me live this life she wanted to be part of; a life she feels entitled to be part of. But she knew how much damage she had done, and she that knew couldn't come back just like things were before. So, she had to find a way to tip toe around to see if there's a chance that I'm willing to help. If I was willing to help her, she would have thought in her mind that she still had a chance to get back in and finish the job of crushing me this time, but I didn't give her that chance. Have I learned my lesson?

You bet I did that. I knew all the tricks and moves that the narcissist pulled, and I wouldn't be fooled again. I've found a way to take all that pain and hurt and turn it into what I've become today. Now, I'm thriving; helping thousands of people to recover and gain insight that would be useful for the rest of their lives. I can tell you that and I am a part of that.

So, who am I? I am Quinn Holiday, a narcissistic survivor who thrives on my experience with a narcissist.

Printed in Great Britain
by Amazon

56794732R00088